ISIS

Goddess of Egypt & India

by
Chris Morgan

Published by
Mandrake of Oxford
PO Box 250
OXFORD
OX1 1AP (UK)

Printed on acid free paper certification from three leading environmental organizations: the Forest Stewardship Council™ (FSC®), the Sustainable Forestry Initiative® (SFI®) and the Programme for the Endorsement of Forestry Certification (PEFC™)

Also by Chris Morgan
Ayurveda: Medicine of the Gods (Basic Principles)

Frontispiece - sanctuary curtain showing Pattini.
Photograph courtesy of Professor Geoffrey Samuel. It was taken in
1998 at a temple in Hanguranketa, near Kandy, Sri Lanka.

Contents

Acknowledgements

Professor Geoffrey Samuel for permission to reproduce his photograph of a sanctuary curtain at a temple in Hanguranketa, near Kandy, Sri Lanka showing Pattini. Thanks also for his many useful articles and leads.

Professor Gunanath Obeyesekere for permission to reproduce, *The Cult of the Goddess Pattini* (Chicago 1984 : pages 245-273) one of the many ritual dramas he transcribed and translated based on his field research in Shri Lanka & South India.

To Dr Richard Fynes whose article: "Isis and Pattini: The Transmission of a Religious Idea from Roman Egypt to India", *JRAS* Series 3.3.3. 1993 : 383 help set me on this quest.

And of course to the goddess Isis, who in a dream requested that I, an otherwise unlikely collaborator, should tell this story. Because of certain events happening in the political sphere just now, it has become difficult to use her name without risking confusion with a terrorist group, which uses a similar acronym. As always I think the goddess will outlive these ephemeral worldly events.

.

Note on transliteration

"Increasingly, scholars writing for a wider audience that is blissfully ignorant of any Indian language have omitted the diacriticals and changed two of the s's to sh (leaving a third s tout court.), *and this book follows that practice.*" *Wendy Doniger The Hindus: an alternative history OUP 2009*

I'm going to do the same, more or less the exception being the accepted spelling of Sri Lanka rather than Shri.

A Temple of Isis in India

On India's south-western or Malabar coast is situated an ancient Hindu temple which is these days devoted to the famous Hindu god Shiva and his consort the fearsome goddess Kali. This is Kurumbha-Bhagavathy Devi outside of the modern city of Cochin or Kochi in Kerala state.

Travel back in time and the temple housed other gods. Once it was the home of the Buddhist/Jaina goddess Pattini whose mortal husband was tried and killed in a series of brutal events still commemorated in the temple's ritual year. Before this and the story gets even stranger, as there are said to be remains of a secret, underground shrine, the home to a mystery cult dedicated to the Egyptian goddess Isis.

At the time of Christ, there was indeed a Greco-Roman merchant colony based in this part of India. Greek, Roman & Near Eastern merchants travelled to India after a regular, if epic, sea journey of two thousand miles across the Arabian Ocean, making their first landfall at a port known in the ancient world as Musiris. Clues to the religious practices of these ancient traders is evident not just in the surviving architecture but in very many, sometimes unique features of the later cults, continuing into the modern day.

Some of the best examples come from the rites of Pattini as once practiced at Kurumba-Bhagavathy Devi. Experts have often identified in the story of her husband's death and resurrection, something of the Near Eastern cult of Attis. But a more recent and credible theory is that the temple once hosted the mysteries of the cult of Isis, whose husband Osiris was also cruelly cut down but then resurrected by her magical prowess.

So without more ado let me tell the whole story from its beginnings on the banks of the Nile. The story of Isis and Osiris is the basis of Egypt's most popular religion. In what follows I trace the origins of this to the Egypt's pyramid age in the middle of the second millennia BCE. Arguably it is even older. A great deal of this book is devoted to describing what is known about the cult of Isis and Osiris from Egyptian records. This, I shall argue, is the basis for what comes later in the time-line, when the world was dominated by the Greek and Roman Empires. Isis and Osiris became the focus of a global religion and the basis of the most popular of all classical mystery cults. This is precisely the time at which a small, Near Eastern shrine was built in South-West India to service the needs of the merchant trading post. Mysteries of Isis were popular amongst all social classes in the ancient world, but especially mariners.

In India we have a building which could itself be thought of as storing the memory of influences from each new wave of belief. We can follow the progress and transformation of its changing occupants, as each absorbs some of the archeological memory. Finally we arrive at its current incarnation and the celebration of the Bharani festival, which marks the beginning of the hot summer before the coming of the Monsoon rains. Many non-orthodox rites will enliven the tale. The mysterious society of Atikals that returns to their lost temple every year to conduct secret rites culminating in twelve hours of 'Misrule', during which hundred of thousands of devotees appear from all over Kerala.

There are other devotees who carry sticks, which they swirl in their dancing; others brandish the sickle sword. Most of these pilgrims are non-Brahmin ritual specialists such as the Veliccappadu. Their name means "a channel who sheds light" for they are spirit mediums, men and women, followers of Kali who utter oracles when in trance. They dress in red and wear heavy anklets and bells.

In the final part of my story I present a complete and 'lost' version of the most famous drama of all time, the celebrated myth or passion play of Isis and murdered husband Osiris, clearly recognizable even in its current idiom based as it is in South Asian ritual drama. The drama is reproduced in its entirety as it reveals many previously unknown aspects of one of the world's oldest myths.

Chris Morgan

Oxford 2016

An Opening Story

Murugan was a Tamil guru of absolute integrity and honesty, great and critical knowledge and a very kind heart.

"Who was your guru?" I asked

He thought about the question for a moment. "My teacher and his teacher before him, and before that all belonged to the line of 'Yakkupo' "

Back then my knowledge of Tamil was rudimentary and the name meant very little to me. I nodded inanely.

"You have never heard of this person?"

I had to admit that I had not.

"Then," he said, "let me translate that into English. Yakkupo is not a Tamil name. What I am saying is that the siddhas of my tradition come from the line of Jacob. Now do you understand?"

I wasn't sure. Could Murugan be talking about a character from the Bible?

"The only Jacob I know about," I said, 'is from the Old Testament."

"Precisely!' he interrupted, "and what do you know about this Jacob?"

I thought for a moment. It had been a long time since I read the Bible. 'Jacob was a patriarch of the Hebrews before they became the nation of Israel."

"Yes."

"Urr," I was searching for a relevant response. Then something I learnt at Sunday school popped into my head, "Jacob", I said rather lamely, "blessed the Pharaoh." [1]

He was the father of Joseph who during a long period of

---

1   Genesis 47:10. 1 Kings 10-11 & 2 Chronicles 9:11 talks
     of King Solomon bringing gold from Ophir which some
     scholars say is India's Malabar coast. In 1 Kings 10:21 the
     "Ships of Tarshish" are mentioned that could be Crete or
     India. See Wendy Doniger, *The Hindus: an alternative
     history*, Oxford 2009 : 338

famine settled his people to Egypt. That the Egyptians could shelter these ancient victims of a great famine is a fact overshadowed by the later accounts of the eventual servitude of the Jews as told in the story of the Exodus. At the end of the *Book of Genesis*. . . "

Murugan now took over the conversation, talking long and excitedly, of how the story of Jacob is full of arcane knowledge of magick and medicine. He reminded me of the skill of Joseph in the interpretation of dreams. Even the story of the *Exodus* was really an account of a magical battle in which the Hebrew priests routed their Egyptian counterparts.

'Yes," I said, it's all coming back to me, but has it really anything to do with the holy men of south India?"

Murugan paused."Well," he said, "it is up to you what you believe. I am merely answering your question. That is where the Siddha doctrine, as taught to me by my teacher, originates. In this I have no doubt. If you have doubts then you must go to your books. But you will find that what I am saying is true. 'Knowledge is like a river, its origins are obscure'."

I told Murugan that I did not doubt what he was saying but that it was the Western way to always seek corroboration. He nodded in agreement.

"Go to your books," he said, "and if I were you I would start by reading about the Romanaka - the Romans."

"The Romans?" I replied, unable to suppress the scepticism in my voice.

"Yes," my guru said, "the Romans. Have you not heard of Sir Mortimer Wheeler?"

I nodded

"The greatest discovery of his life was the presence of the Romans here in this part of India. You will see."

And so I did.

The Tamil Siddhas

The eminent Tamil scholar Professor Kamil Zvelebil was one of the first to record the extremely heterodox beliefs of the south Indian sadhus.[1] In Tamil Nadu these people are members of secret societies called Siddhas. Siddhas are holy men and women, followers of a pan-Indian mystical tradition. These people are beyond the traditional strictures of caste and class. Their rites are strange and include much that we would call magick or witchcraft. These people have their own definitions of the meaning of social class. And these traditions are about as far away as it is possible to get from the po-faced priests of traditional Hinduism.

Gods made out of wood[2]
Gods made out of stone
Gods made out of palmyra fronds
Gods made out of bone
Gods made out of rags
Gods made out of dung
Gods made out of saffron bags
There are no other gods
but - THE VOID

---

1   Kamil V Zvelebil, *The Poets of the Powers*, Rider 1973.
2   Civavakkiyam 503/510 in Kamil V Zvelebil, *The Siddha Quest for Immortality*, Mandrake 2003

They also acknowledge the existence of several international sodalities of magi, including one called 'The Ekiptaya' by which they mean the Egyptians.

Where do these ideas originate? Are they a 'modern' invention? When I set out to investigate the origins of this tradition I had little idea where it would lead me. I came upon a story, largely buried in academic journals that was extremely fascinating in its own right. I discovered a theme that seemed to provide a unique insight into Indian culture. As the great mythographer Mircea Eliade wrote: 'There is no more absorbing story than that of the discovery and interpretation of India by Western consciousness.'[1]

But the reward was to be even greater. The survival of a truly Egyptian magical tradition in India, opens up new possibilities of understanding ancient Egypt and its religion. The odd twist of history that brought both the Egyptian and Indian cultures together in such a direct way, enables us to apply the comparative method in which light will be shed on both traditions. For example the facts presented in this book fill important gaps in a tradition that has come to be known as Hermetic.

Hermeticism is syncretic or a bricolage religion, whose central tenets came together in Alexandria; the ancient city

---

1.   Mircea Eliade, *Yoga, Immortality & Freedom*, 1958 : 27

founded by Alexander the Great in the Nile Delta. To call Hermeticism or magick a religion is controversial, the arguments for this are summarized in my book *Phi-Neter: Power of the Egyptian Gods*. Hermeticism combines elements of Egyptian theology, their gods and goddesses with other religious themes totally alien to that land. In the early centuries after Christ, Hermeticism was steadily suppressed. With a few important exceptions, the body of Hermetic knowledge was, as far as we know, lost and forgotten until it began to re-emerge in the European Renaissance fifteen hundred years after its disappearance from history. Hermeticism was lost, or so it seems, when one of those 'dark ages' descended upon human intellectual history. The end of Egypt coincides with the temporary disappearance of the Hermetic philosophy, which nevertheless became part of several other religious traditions.

Our story, in part, traces what happened to ancient religious traditions and doctrines, when, to use a rather poetic metaphor, the lights in the sanctuary were extinguished. For as it happens, at the time of Christ, there was a Greco-Roman merchant colony in south India. These merchants arrived in India after a regular if epic sea journey of two thousand miles across the Arabian Ocean making their first landfall at a port known in the ancient world as Musiris.

The old port had changed its name several times until 1431

when it silted up altogether. From that time onwards, Cochin replaced it as the region's main harbour. These days the urbanized site is known as *Kotunkolur*.

Although Roman speculators usually bankrolled the ancient maritime trade, Greek seamen almost invariably navigated the ships. Those Greek mariners, often natives of Alexandria, invariably worshipped the Egyptian goddess Isis. The cult of Isis had by then become a world religion, with very many devotees all around the Mediterranean and beyond. Isis was particularly important as the protector of people on dangerous sea voyages.

Isis was said to have many names, and one of them, as I shall prove in this book, is the Tamil goddess Pattini, the guardian deity of Sri Lanka who was once also worshipped by the Hindus and Buddhists of South India. Back then Pattini was a composite Jaina-Buddhist deity. A central feature of her mythology concerns the killing and death of her husband Palanga; her search for him; her role as *mater dolorosa* weeping over his corpse and her power to resurrect him, albeit temporarily. This resurrection motif is hardly found anywhere else in the Hindu tradition, with the possible exception of the myth of Savitri as found in the MahaBharata.[1]

---

1. *Mahabharata* III 291-298. The following passage from M M Ganguli's 1883 edition accessed 2015 http:// www.sacred-texts.com/hin/m03/m03291.htm.

Here's the story from the *Mahabharata*, a text whose historical frame is difficult to place but which some say could record some of the dynastic struggles of South India:

The old king of Madras being childless received as a boon from the goddess Savitri, a daughter beautiful enough to be her incarnation. At puberty she was beautiful and he sent her out to look for a husband amongst forest dwelling communities. There she found a young man called Satyavan "great soul" or occasionally he is called Chitaashva "drawer of horses" because of his skill in sketching horses. He is of noble birth, the child of a former deposed king, who had retired to the forest to pursue a religious life in an hermitage. This whole scenario sounds very like a typical Buddhist or Jaina milieu.

The only fault of this perfect youth was that he was destined to live but one more year. The match was agree and Savitri moved to the forest retreat to live an ascetic life with her new husband and family. She dresses in clothes made of birch bark dyed red. On the fateful last day of his life, she goes with her husband foraging in the forest. He becomes weak and sleeps. As she guards him, a fearsome god, also dressed in red, appears holding a noose. This is Yama, god of the dead, lord of *pitris* or spirits who, rather than sending his emissaries, has come in person to claim the soul of Satyavan. This he has done because this is a great soul.

Yama then pulls the life (the Jiva) from his body, which becomes lifeless and unsightly. The *jiva* is the size of his thumb. He takes it to the south. But Savitri follows Yama, keeping precisely seven paces behind him, which causes Yama to ask her why she is following.

Thus he learns of devotion and as a reward he grants her a miracle, offering to cure the blindness of her father-in-law. Yama is able to offer this as he is a creature of fire, the very element which is thought to be connected with sight. Obviously not satisfied, Savitri continues to follow, several times engaging the lord of death in discussion and each time impressing him sufficiently by her merits for him to grant her a succession of boons. Thus she earns five miracles culminating in the restoration of her husband.

Returning to the story of Pattini, at Kotunkolur near Cochin there is an ancient temple which has the remains of a secret underground shrine which, so I intend to argue, was originally dedicated to her ancient cult. This temple has seen many changes since it was first founded at the time of Christ. In the Indian middle ages (circa 9th century in the modern calendar) Hinduism became the largest religion of the region and Buddhism and Jainism disappeared. Hinduism itself experienced a series of reforms, initiated coincidentally by a former Buddhist, called Shankara, who was born in Kotunkolur. The original rites were discontinued or driven underground. A purely Hindu goddess called Kali, replaced Pattini. Even so, some of the original descendants of the Isis worshippers managed to hang on through the changes and are still to this day preserve connection to the temple although not as priests (pujaris) but as administrators.

The Opening of the Ways

This remarkable survival of Egyptian ideas transferred to this South India temple was only possibly due to an equally remarkable feat of navigation. The beginnings of contact between India and the Middle East is lost in the mists of ancient history or even prehistory. We need only look to the writings of Greek philosopher Plato (428-348BCE) for evidence of ancient connections. In his books there is a description of a medical system that has been identified as an early account of Indian Ayurveda!

"A third class of diseases we must conceive as arising in three ways: one by the agency of air, the second by phlegm, the third of bile."[1]

The three humours or *doshas* of Ayurveda are Vata, Pitta & Kapha, often translated as Air, Phlegm and Bile.

In 336BCE, a few years after Plato's death, Alexander, a Macedonian, largely unknown outside of his native land,

---

1.   Plato, *Timaeus* 84d-86a, Translated by Benjamin Jowett

ascended the throne of his murdered father Philip. Macedonia was a province of Northern Greece but it soon became the hub of an international empire stretching from Egypt to the banks of the river Indus. Alexander's conquest of the North Western reaches of the Indian sub-continent (modern day Pakistan), in the fourth century before Christ established a land bridge.

Take a look at a modern map and think of the geopolitics of this route. The road into the north west of India via Afghanistan is dangerous today and it was hardly less so in ancient times. For those who travelled the land bridge between east and west, it was long, hard, expensive and dangerous. Alexander's famous 'retreat' from India, later established a coastal route. Ships soon retraced his journey which for safety reasons they sailed strictly within sight of the land. Consequently all cargoes were 'taxed' as they entered the coastal waters of the many small kingdoms that ringed the coast. Mediterranean merchant ships could in this manner reach the rich marts of the extreme South of India but it was a very long voyage often of more than two years duration. Sometimes these ships never returned. This is hardly an attractive investment for a Roman entrepreneur!

Even so, the Romans wanted to buy diamonds, pearls, sapphires, agate, onyx, rubies, ivory and muslins. They also wanted Chinese silks, Indian cottons, peacocks, large tigers for the amphitheatre, carnelian, cardamom and above all pepper. The Romans were particularly fond of pepper. Indeed so much did a taste for this precious commodity spread to the rest of their empire, that even Alaric the Goth demanded 3,000lbs of pepper in his treaty with the Romans of AD408. [1]

Pepper was more than a culinary herb, its excellent medicinal qualities had been described in Ayurvedic Indian medicine for millennia. The kingdoms in South India were particularly rich in these commodities and the Romans with their Greek vessels regularly plied their trade here along what is termed the Malabar coast.

The journey may be long but the rewards were sufficiently great to make it just viable to follow the long route, coasting around the rim of the Arabian/Indian Ocean. Port taxes, nowadays called *cabotage*, were steep and probably too frequent. But the bottom line was that at journey's end the ship's cargo would provide more than enough profit to make the whole enterprise worth while. Before the 21st year of the common era, the historian Pliny estimated that 120 ships had made the trip. [2]

---

1.   Mortimer Wheeler, *My Archaeological Mission to India and Pakistan.* (Thames & Hudson 1976 : 55)

2.   Legendary King Solomon sent ships every three years. See footnote page 8 above.

Although the South of India was never part of the Roman Empire, the Romans established several trading stations on its Western (*Malabar*) and Eastern (*Coromandel*) Coasts. With the benefit of modern maps we can see that there is a direct route across the Arabian Ocean to the prosperous trading centres of the South. But the journey is one of more than 2000 miles of open ocean.

During the rulership of Roman emperor Augustus (23BCE - CE14) there are records of visits to Rome of at least two Indian delegations. Soon after this visit or perhaps later during the reign of Claudius, Greek navigators confirmed the existence of the direct route to south India. Only during the reign of Augustus was maritime technology sufficiently well organized to make the open ocean route a viable one. It took advantage of a monsoon wind that came later to be known as 'hippalos', a Greek personal name and therefore assumed to be that of an early nautical pioneer. Using this wind, a trading ship could, in forty days, sail directly across the ocean from Ocelis, in modern Aden, to the ancient port of Musiris, near to what is today the city of Cochin in modern Kerala.

Two monsoon systems, a south-western & north-eastern, dominate the Arabian sea. The south west monsoon would bring ships from the Red Sea to India's western or Malabar coast. Stormy wet winds started in May and were calm enough from August to November, to be conducive for sailing. The north-eastern winds begin in October; and from January to May, provided good sailing from India, faring eastwards to the Red Sea.[1] Armed with this knowledge, merchant ships, having sold their cargo of copper, lead, tin, wine, slaves, silver and gold coins, could sail back, making landfall at Ocelis (Aden) on the Arabian coast. From there is was a relatively straightforward trip to the Red Sea port of Berenice where the cargo could be taken across the desert to be reloaded onto Nile ships for transport to Alexandria and thence onward to Rome.

A skilled navigator, with knowledge of this pattern of ocean winds could make the hardest part of the journey in forty days. When the pioneers had done their work, the route became as predictable and therefore as safe as crossing the Mediterranean itself. The great scholar Professor Kamil Zvelebil has written a lively account of the impact of one of these early speculative voyages. As this trade wind still bears the ancient Greek name 'Hippalos', Professor Zvelebil, exercising some poetic licence, gave the name 'Hippalos' to the novel's central character, the vessel's Alexandrian captain.

---

1. Sean McGrail *Early Ships and Seafaring: Water Transport Beyond Europe,* 2015 : 47-8]

The Tamil language has many words borrowed from Europe. And in turn there are many words in Greek, Latin and even Semitic tongues derived from Asian technical terms. In linguistics these are known generically as loan words. So for example the Indian term 'Yavana' or 'Yonaka' in the following passage is Greek 'Ionian'.

'Muziris, the great Chera mart, and the main sea-port of the ancient kingdom of the Cheres, on the western coast of southern India, always lively, always crowded, never dull, never quiet, was on that particular day in the grip of feverish excitement. Along the banks of the river Periyar lingered groups of tired harbor serfs, filling their bellies with turtle fat enjoying the roasted flesh of lampreys, and flushing that heavy treat down with strong, hot palm wine. They were probably the only ones who failed to be thrilled by what was happening that late afternoon out on the sea. On the mole, on the pier, and along the shore, throngs and crowds of dark-skinned men, women and children were watching the monstrous apparition of a huge ship which was emerging from behind the horizon; in a straight line ahead towards the West, where the endless ocean spread out from India into unknown, unseen regions. Bullock-carts along the paved roads stopped, palanquins and sedan-chairs were lowered onto the sand, still warm, and even the light, swift chariots stood immobile, their passengers watching the approaching sea-monster. An elephant, halted in its progress, knelt down expecting its mahout to descend, but the man preferred to remain sitting in the howdah, since from the elevated post of observation he had a better view of what was happening.

'A pirate!'

'Nonsense. Pirate boats are smaller and faster.'

'I say a pirate from Nitra.'

'What a monster!'

'Huge, isn't she? Must be a Yavana vessel!'

'A Yavana vessel? Rubbish! They always come coasting from the North.'

'I told you, it's a pirate from the islands.'

'No, it's not a pirate, it's a *makara* fish, a leviathan, a whale!'

Laughter all around at the attempted joke. Then: 'look - look, I can see the mastheads now! One, two - three! It's a ship of the Romanakas! It must be!'

Now they could see it was a Yavana ship, incredibly large, with three masts, and, what was utterly unexpected, it approached the port of Musiri straight from across the seas, not, as usual, from the northern quarter along the narrow coastline of the Chera kingdom, what even then was called Keralam.

Alexandria to Coptos, from Coptos to Berenice, from Berenice to Ocelis and then, on July 15, from Ocelis at the southern tip of Arabia straight across the Mare Erythraeum.

The above is a fictionalized account of the arrival in India of Roman & Greek traders. It is a big story in itself but what I intend to concentrate on is the religious beliefs of the newcomers, in particular the goddess Isis, whom they certainly venerated and transported to India.[1]

The Goddess Isis

The Egyptian Goddess Isis had already travelled a long way from her antique origins before she ever set foot on those Roman ships. Isis is remarkable in several ways. To many historians and modern devotees she is "The Great Goddess" who has been with us since the beginning of time. But the story of Isis did not always look so grand. Her origins may in fact be more "humble" but no less venerable and magical for that.

---

1. *The Roman Empire and the Indian Ocean: the ancient world economy & the kingdoms of Africa, Arabia & India*, Raoul McLaughlin 2014

She may once have been an spiritual entity connected with the home, where she was an ancestral spirit who was invoked during the period of mourning for the dead. In the pharaonic, high culture which came after these early, archaic mindsets, she was given a new form and a new name. The texts that record this process arguably hint at her original name which may well have been: Heaet (*ḥȝt*):

> The Heaet (HAt) bird comes, the Djeret (Drt) bird comes; this is Isis with Nephthys. They come seeking their brother Osiris.[1]

The descriptions of the deeds of Isis in the so-called Pyramid texts furnish the earliest known archaeological evidence for her worship. These are still Egypt's oldest known religious literature. These texts are inscribed on the walls of the first Pyramids and are therefore usually dated to about 2400-2300BCE? It is likely that the religious myths contained in these texts were developed by the priesthood sometime before they were carved in stone. The Pyramid texts are a window not just on Isis but on a wider cult that included her famous husband Osiris. The texts themselves seem to refer back to an older solar cult that was known to the scribes from an older, pre-existent manuscript tradition.

---

1. *The Ancient Egyptian Pyramid Texts,* translated by R O Faulkner, *OUP 1969:* 1280b-c

We cannot really understand the goddess Isis unless we look in detail at her husband Osiris. This is because for the first few thousand years of its existence, Osiris was the most important thing in her life, her cult. It is only in later times, and by that I mean those of the Romans and Greeks, that the goddess Isis becomes more important than her husband.

The Cult of Osiris

The Pyramid texts contain many passages referring to the cult of Osiris but a complete or "canonical" version of the myth is most easily read in texts that are actually written 1500years later. This is the time of the 18th dynasty (circa 1500BCE). The 18th dynasty contains many of the most famous, to us, of all ancient Egyptians, including among them are the female Pharaoh Hatshepsut and the heretic king Akhenaten.

The "Great Hymn of Osiris" or "Hymn of Amenmose" is our primary source. Amenmose was not a king but a minor court official. His funeral stela (see picture) is of fine construction, in the lunette above the extensive text he is shown together with his family. Here's an extract:[1]

Praise to thee, Osiris! Thou lord of eternity, king of gods! Thou

1.   Source: A Erman (2006) *Ancient Egyptian Literature*, Routledge p141-145; translated from German by Aylward M. Blackman also M Lichtheim

with many names and lordly of being! With mysterious ceremonies in the temples.

Noteworthy here is possible reference to the existence of a mystery cult functioning in the god's temples. The existence of mystery cults in ancient Egypt is controversial and denied by some authorities. The eminent Erik Hornung seems put out that his colleague Jan Assmann "who is otherwise not inclined toward esoteric interpretations sees "secret Hermetic wisdom" and a "sort of cabala" in the Books of the Netherworld from the Royal tombs."[1]

Returning to our text one reads:

The firmament and its stars hearken unto him, and the great portals open to him; to whom men shout for joy in the southern sky, whom men adore in the northern sky.

This passage above is an allusion to death and resurrection of the God Osiris. We know this from reading similar passages in so-called *Books of Afterlife* such as *The Book of Gates*, where the progress of Osiris through the Underworld to resurrection at dawn is clearly mapped out against the night sky.

The imperishable stars are under his authority, and the never

1.   Erik Hornung *The Secret Lore of Egypt*, Cornell 2001 : 184

The Stele of Amenmose, sources of the Great Hymn of Osiris. Louvre
(C286) published by Alexandre Moret BIFAO 30 (1931) p 750

wearying ones are his place of abode.

The "imperishable stars" are the Northern circumpolar constellations in which Egyptian gods were thought to dwell, although rather confusingly Osiris also has a strong association with the Southern constellation Orion.

> *Offerings are made to him by the command of Geb, and the Nine Gods adore him; they that are in the Underworld kiss the ground, and they that are in the necropolis make an obeisance. The [deceased] shout for joy when they behold him, they that are there are in fear of him. The two lands together give him praise at the approach of his majesty.*

> *He that established right throughout the Two River-banks and placed the son upon his father's seat praised of his father Geb; beloved of his mother Nuit.*

This allusion here is to the important *Heliopolitan* cosmology, one of several ways at looking at the origins of the gods and humanity. In this version the earth god Geb and the sky mother Nuit are the parents of four gods, two couples viz. Isis and Osiris; Seth & Nephthys.

> *The heir of Geb in the kingship of the Two Lands. He saw how excellent he was, and he entrusted it to him to lead the Two Lands to good fortune.*

Because Isis & Osiris were born before Seth & Nephthys

they have the legal status conferred by primogeniture and ought by natural right to inherit the kingdom of their father Geb.

He placed this land in his hand, its water and its air, its crops and its cattle. All that flieth and all that fluttereth, its worms and its wild beasts, were made over to the son of Nuit, and the two Lands were contented therewith...His sister protected him.

But things do not go smoothly and their status is contested. The issue was new because all previous generations of gods had been one male with one female. There is nothing self-evidently valid in the plea to primogeniture, indeed it all coincides with the rise or emergence of the institution of kingship. Perhaps in earlier ages things were different and other ways of managing inheritance of wealth and titles were the norm.

The second born son Seth is jealous of his older brother and eventually makes a murderous assault in a manner familiar to us from later myths such as that of Cain & Abel. This is too taboo for the ancient poet to dwell upon in detail. He merely tells us that the goddess Isis tries to "protect" her husband/brother Osiris, although she is really only able to protect his corpse and his legacy.

She that held the foes aloof and warded off the deeds of the miscreant by the beneficent things of her mouth, she of the excellent tongue, whose words come not to nought, and admirable to command.

The god Seth is here called the *miscreant*. The reference to "beneficent words of her mouth" is taken to mean the goddess's well-known use of magic and the related power of words.

Beneficent Isis, that protected her brother, that sought for him without wearying, that traversed this land mourning, and took no rest until she found him.

Isis searches and eventually finds the corpse of Osiris, which Seth has dismembered and left floating in the Nile, until the current swept it down to the Delta.

She that afforded him shade with her feathers, and with her wings created air. She that cried aloud for joy and brought her brother to land.

Here the hymn describes Isis in her most popular form, personified as a kite, the bird of mourning. As a bird she searches for the corpse from the air, then protects it, fanning air into Osiris with her wings.

She that revived the faintness of the Weary One, that took in his seed, and provided an heir, that suckled the child in solitude, the place where he was being unknown, that brought him, when his arm was strong, into the hall of Geb.

Although Osiris is dead, Isis manages through her uncanny powers to revive him. This is the unique aspect of their myth that is the model for many later stories of dying and resurrecting gods, including a special example from India. Osiris is revived just long enough to conceive an heir, the god Horus. Some also see this as a miraculous or even virgin birth. She is virgin because up to this point Isis has no other children, and conception is not by the normal way. We shall return to this theme later where it is amplified in later mystery cults.

Horus is a falcon god & therefore shares the avian form of his mother rather than the anthropoid form of his father. This provides further reason why Seth can dispute the inheritance of Horus. It is also the reason Horus needs to be hidden from his uncle Seth until he is old enough to return to the court of his grandfather Geb and claim his "birthright". Only when he is a fully grown and powerful adult has he any hope of avenging the murder of his father Osiris.

The Ennead cried out full of joy:
"Welcome, Horus, son of Osiris!
Stalwart hearted, justified!
Son of Isis, heir of Osiris!"

The ancient narrative gets a little ahead of itself, anticipating the outcome of a tribunal of all the gods that must decide if Horus does have a valid claim to the throne of his father. His paternity is never in doubt, which strikes us as odd given what has happened. Could the ancestry of his mother Isis play a role in the tribunal's decision, perhaps a survival of ancient matrilineal law codes?

The Tribunal of Truth assembled for him, the Ennead and the Lord of All himself, the lords of truth that were united therein, that turned their backs on iniquity.

The tribunal of all the gods sat down in the hall of Geb with the intent to assign the office to its lord, the kingdom to whom it should be given.

It was found that the word of Horus was true, and the office of his father was given unto him. He came forth crowned by the command of Geb, he received the Lordship of the Two Riverbanks, and the crown rested securely on his head.

The assumption of kingship by Horus rests solely on the word of his mother Isis, that she gave birth to him and that his father was Osiris. In ancient laws of succession the lineage did in fact pass to the son of the first wife of the reigning king rather than to the second in line to the throne. Horus, whilst still a child, must prove he is able to rule.

As I mentioned earlier, other than the presentation of these myths in the Pyramid texts, there is surprisingly little archaeological evidence for the existence of a cult of Osiris or his consort Isis for the era before the pyramids were built.

There are no temples or shrines, no statues or dedications. If Isis had any prehistoric cult centres in Egypt, their whereabouts are as yet unknown. Her main cult places in later times were Behbet el Hagar in the Delta, which was not even founded until 380BCE. Older centres are evidenced at Akhmin, at Coptos, and most famous of all at Philae. All of these are of a comparatively late date in the very long and sustained tradition of Egyptian temple building.

This absence from the archaeological record needs to be explained. It seems possible that Isis & Osiris were not part of the oldest strata of belief or if they were, they were parts of other constellations of gods. The scribes, have obviously been up to a bit of myth making, rearranging all the characters of older times and composing a totally new drama.

We can still see some of the joins in this ancient cut and paste exercise. Horus, the Falcon God was, indeed he is one of the oldest of all Egyptian gods. As is the "miscreant" god Set or Seth, who was originally paired with Horus not as "wicked uncle" but as his Brother! The Cow Goddess Hathor; the obliging grandmother Neith, all have ancient antecedents. Indeed all of the actors in the myth of Isis & Osiris possess ample archaeological evidence of an ancient life, apart that is from the principal golden couple. This and other obvious inconsistencies throw doubt on the extreme antiquity of the myth. Although for most of us it is as old as it needs to be.

The situation is complex because Isis then takes over many of the attributes of older goddesses such as Hathor. It therefore seems highly likely that the rise of the cult of Isis & Osiris can be traced to a particular event, much as we might ascribe a date to the birth of the Christian or Muslim faith. One such obvious political event was the unification of the whole land of Egypt under one ruler. The myth of divine kingship enters the discourse at that very same moment along with several other innovations including the abandonment of the archaic lunar ritual calendar, replaced by the 360+5 days solar year that is so linked with the Osirian cult.

Archaeologists are steadily assembling a great deal of information about Egypt's ancient origins. The people who eventually became the Egyptians once lived in what is now the arid Sahara desert. For a brief time in the late neolithic, part of the desert were green and fertile land and a prehistoric culture developed beside a great lake. But ecological changes caused this lake to desiccate forcing the people to move. They came to the banks of the Nile. Their familiarity with the ecology of periodic floods helped them manage the Nile's annual inundation. They saw how the flood resolved itself into a series of 42 temporary lakes (coincidentally or perhaps not but 42 is an important symbolic number, it is for example the number of judges in the Underworld.) Each of these 42 lakes supported a different tribe and was as a consequence represented by a special fetish or totem.

Nome standard of 21st Upper Egyptian nome

When the climatic conditions in the Nile valley worsened, some individuals must have proved themselves more skilled at managing the food supply, ensuring there were resources in good times and bad. This is rather like the myth of Joseph and the famines of Egypt as 'remembered' in the Bible. It is posited that these natural cycles provided opportunities for some family clans to accumulate wealth and resources. This situation provided an opportunity for someone to show leadership and in it perhaps lies the origin of the chieftain, who later became a local king and eventually a single king unifying all under his or sometime her rule.

It is only after all these changes that the mature myth of Isis and Osiris comes into the world. This leads some to ask whether the story of Isis & Osiris is "true myth". A true myth would be one that has mystical, numinous origins rather than being some kind of scribal or political construction. John Gwyn-Griffiths is the great scholarly expert on this material, and has translated many of the classic sources, principally *Plutarch*'s *Isis & Osiris*. Here he writes that "The myth appears thus to dissolve itself into a story built around a set of ceremonies in which the dead king is the centre. This does not mean that it is not a *true myth* of a particular kind; it must be categorized as one of those which are engendered by ritual although it also draws upon the mythology already attached to the protagonists – in the case the living king who is Horus." [1]

Isis and her sister Nephthys are often called the two *kites*. Kites are raptors who eat carrion, usually small mammals. The Egyptologist Siegfried Schott has suggested that these birds were symbols of mourning long before they were identified with goddesses such as Isis and Nephthys. [2] So Isis must originally have been a representation of the mourner at an archaic funeral, mimicking the gathering of birds, especially the vultures that sometimes circle and wait to devour a fresh corpse. This marks the beginning of a long

---

1. Gwyn Griffiths, *The Origins of Osiris & His Cult*, Brill *(1980 : 35) who cites* R. Anthes *JNES 18 (1959) 208)* on the origin of myth in ritual connected with death of the King.

2. Quoted in Gwyn-Griffiths *(1970: 49)*

association between birds and the ominous, a commonplace of folklore the world over.

Kites are not known as devourers of whole corpses of large animals, although human dead are routinely eaten by vultures. It is possible that the Kite, because of its distinctive screeching, became associated with the keening of mourners. Or indeed the keening of mourners may be borrowed from the behaviour of birds.

These are very ancient beliefs. One can perhaps see how the bare facts of the disposal of the dead in the Stone Ages might over time have evolved into a ritual exposure of the body to be eaten by scavengers such as the jackal or vulture. This returning of the flesh to the biosphere naturally leads to the idea of the vulture as mother of new life.

In her book, *Isis Magic: Cultivating the goddess with a thousand names*,[1] M Isadora Forrest makes a connection between Isis and the supposed "Bird of Prey Goddesss" of Çatal Hoyuk. In this she is following the contested theories of anthropologist Marija Gimbutas, especially *The Language of the Goddess*.[2] This remarkable ancient settlement in Turkey

---

1. M Isadora Forrest, *Isis Magic: Cultivating the goddess with a thousand names* (Llewellyn 2001 : 24sq)

2. Marija Gimbutas, *The Language of the Goddess: unearthing the hidden symbols of western civilization* (Thames & Hudson 1989).

was occupied between 7500BCE to 5700BCE. It was partially excavated in the 1960s and restarted in the 1990s directed by Ian Hodder. The work of Gimbutas was based on the earlier discoveries, many of the theories about a supposed ancient goddess culture at the site have been considerably amended by the newer discoveries.

At Çatal Hoyuk there are indeed depictions of vultures devouring headless corpses. But is there any obvious sign that these vultures are female? Whether they are female or goddesses is really a little uncertain. These scenes come from inside domestic houses, under whose floors the inhabitants also buried their dead. It is not unlikely that these images have something to do with transcendence - the transformation of something from one state to another.

Isis assumes this bird form when performing one of her most important roles. In the words of Amenmose: "She that afforded him shade with her feathers, and with her wings created air. She that cried aloud for joy and brought her brother to land. She that revived the faintness of the Weary One, that took in his seed, and provided an heir." She does not take this form in any other context. This then is her most primal role, a launchpad from which she accumulates a number of other functions within Egyptian religion.

One might ask, as does J Gwyn-Griffiths "Why the two goddesses [Isis & Nephthys] would be imagined as birds in this particular function of [guarding the dead Osiris] and only in this function."[1]

He continues "other goddesses are mentioned as fulfilling a similar function but the emergence of Isis and Nephthys as the constant actors of the role is perhaps part of the triumph [of] . . . the Osirian cult." Gwyn Griffiths thought this identification was really a reflection of the power of the falcon god Horus,[2] the divine counterpart of the living King. The rise of Isis occurs as the same time as the emergence of this idea of divine kingship. It is as well to remind ourselves that the institution of kingship is an innovation of historic times. The iconography of Isis shows her with a hieroglyph above or on her head. This hieroglyph is a stylized throne. The name Isis could literally be interpreted as meaning the throne - which some see as evidence of royal descent being somehow dependent of the female line?

The connection of Isis to the cult of divine kingship is exemplified by another of her avatars - the Uraeus or spitting cobra who sits upon the royal diadem as the ultimate protector of the king.

1.   J Gwyn Griffiths, *The Origins of Osiris and his cult*, Brill 1980 : 49

2.   Gwyn Griffiths, 1980: 50

Vulture pecking at decapitated corpses, fresco discussed in Ian Hodder Çatal Hoyuk: The Leopard's tale revealing the mysteries of Turkey's ancient 'town', Thames & Hudson 2006

"Through twin doors of the horizon, It is the dawn
When holy serpents fly and two cobras lie
Isis & her sister Nephthys, Those who light for Ra
going after this god, Into mysterious Door of the West."
Book of Gates, 12th Hour [1]

In the Roman era this serpent form is further extended to absorb an ancient deity connected with the harvest - Renenutet, known then as Thermoutis and paired with Serapis - a late form of Osiris.

---

1. Rodgers, *Contemporary Western Book of the Dead* (Mandrake 2012 : 178)

Another major change in her role takes place in the New Kingdom when she assimilates the symbolism of the ancient cow goddess Hathor. According to Francesco Tiradritti "this represents the beginning of her liberation from the cult of Osiris, and emergence as a deity in her own right." [1]

The goddess Hathor has a long prehistoric pedigree. She is similar if not the same goddess as the dis-embodied BAT, meaning "female soul" shown on one of Egypt's oldest and most important artefacts - the ceremonial Narmer palette of the 31st century BCE.

Decapitation or being dis-embodied is an extremely ancient funeral practice. We are so used to seeing portrait busts that we have forgotten to remember that this is no mere artistic convention. The absence of the body in divine images such as those of Bat, Hathor, Bes etc is quite deliberate and recalls a cult focussed on the head. Bat's origins also lead us back to a prehistoric cattle cult. In a mythological episode, Isis literally takes or is given the head of a cow to replace one her son Horus has loped off in a rage! From this point on Isis retains her anthropoid form but with a crown of cow's horns and a solar disk.

---

1.   *Catalogue of exhibition*, curator Carla Maria Burri "Isis, The Egyptian Goddess that Conquered Rome" Egyptian Museum of Cairo 1998 : 4

Classic image of Isis standing behind King Ramesses III

Hathor is variously the patroness of music, alcohol and sexuality. Hathor and Isis represent two important female types. Hathor is said to instantiate the more *antisocial* side of female sexuality. Hathor is more about non procreative sex whereas Isis is the archetype of the ideal Egyptian woman. Her eroticism is sometimes more conventional than that of Hathor. She is loyal and faithful to her divine husband Osiris even beyond death. Isis also takes Hathor's most famous magical "accessory", a rattle called a sistrum. She also assumes the ritual container known as a situla (Egyptian *wšb*), a breast shaped pot or bucket used to make libations of cow's milk. This association is particularly interesting for the Indian cult of Pattini to be discussed below.

Isis also absorbs the fecund aspect of Hathor, even exploiting her relationship with the sun god Ra and at the same time giving it this interesting twist:

The Legend of Ra and Isis

Now Isis was a woman who possessed words of power; her heart was wearied with the millions of men, and she chose the millions of the gods, but she esteemed more highly the

Image of BAT, "Female Soul", detail from Narmer Palette, circa 3100bce

millions of spirits (*akhw*). And she meditated in her heart, saying, "Cannot I by means of the sacred name of God make myself mistress of the earth and become a goddess like unto 'Ra in heaven and upon earth?' "

Now, behold, each day Ra entered at the head of his holy mariners and established himself upon the throne of the two horizons. The holy one had grown old, he dribbled at the mouth, his spittle fell upon the earth, and his slobbering dropped upon the ground. And Isis kneaded it with earth in her hand, and formed thereof a sacred serpent in the form of a spear; she set it not upright before her face, but let it lie upon the ground in the path whereby the great god went forth, according to his heart's desire, into his double kingdom. Now the holy god arose, and the gods who followed him as though he were Pharaoh went with him; and he came forth according to his daily wont; and the sacred serpent bit him. The flame of life departed from him, and he who dwelt among the cedars (?) was overcome. The holy god opened his mouth, and the cry of his majesty reached unto heaven. His company of gods said, "What hath happened?" and his gods exclaimed, "What is it?" But Ra could not answer, for his jaws trembled and all his members quaked; the poison spread swiftly through his flesh just as the Nile invadeth all his land.

When the great god had stablished his heart, he cried unto

Image of Hathor blessing the King with her gold

those who were in his train, saying, "Come unto me, O ye who have come into being from my body, ye gods who have come forth from me, make ye known unto Khepera that a dire calamity hath fallen upon me. My heart perceiveth it, but my eyes see it not; my hand hath not caused it, nor do I know who hath done this unto me. Never have I felt such pain, neither can sickness cause more woe than this. I am a prince, the son of a prince, a sacred essence which hath preceded from God. I am a great one, the son of a great one, and my father planned my name; I have multitudes of names and multitudes of forms, and my existence is in every god.

I have been proclaimed by the heralds Tum and Horus, and my father and my mother uttered my name; but it hath been hidden within me by him that begat me, who would not that the words of power of any seer should have dominion over me. I came forth to look upon that which I had made, I was passing through the world which I had created, when lo! something stung me, but what I know not. Is it fire? Is it water? My heart is on fire, my flesh quaketh, and trembling hath seized all my limbs. Let there be brought unto me the children of the gods with healing words and with lips that know, and with power which reacheth unto heaven."

The children of every god came unto him in tears, Isis came with her healing words and with her mouth full of the breath of life, with her enchantments which destroy sickness, and with her words of power which make the dead to live. And she spoke, saying, "What has come to pass, O holy father? What has happened? A serpent has bitten thee, and a thing which thou created has lifted up his head against thee. Verily it shall be cast forth by my healing words of power, and I will drive it away from before the sight of thy sunbeams."

The holy god opened his mouth and said, "I was passing along my path, and I was going through the two regions of my lands according to my heart's desire, to see that which I had created, when lo! I was bitten by a serpent which I saw not. Is it fire? Is it water? I am colder than water, I am hotter than fire. All my flesh sweats, I quake, my eye has no strength, I cannot see the sky, and the sweat rushes to my face even as in the time of summer."

Then said Isis unto Ra, "O tell me thy name, holy father, for whosoever shall be delivered by thy name shall live." [And Ra said], "I have made the heavens and the earth, I have ordered the mountains, I have created all that is above them, I have made the water, I have made to come into being the great and wide sea, I have made the 'Bull of his mother,' from whom spring the delights of love. I have made the heavens, I have stretched out the two horizons like a curtain, and I have placed the soul of the gods within them. I am he who, if he openeth his eyes, doth make the light, and, if he closeth them, darkness cometh into being. At his command the Nile riseth, and the gods know not his name. I have made the hours, I have created the days, I bring forward the festivals of the year, I create the Nile-flood. I make the fire of life, and I provide food in the houses. I am Khepera in the morning, I am Ra at noon, and I am Tum at evening."

Meanwhile the poison was not taken away from his body, but it pierced deeper, and the great god could no longer walk.

Then said Isis unto Ra, "What thou hast said is not thy name. O tell it unto me, and the poison shall depart; for he shall live whose name shall be revealed." Now the poison burned like fire, and it was fiercer than the flame and the furnace, and the majesty of the god said, "I consent that Isis shall search into me, and that my name shall pass from me into her."

Then the god hid himself from the gods, and his place in the boat of millions of years was empty. And when the time arrived for the heart of Ra to come forth, Isis spake unto her son Horus, saying, "The god hath bound himself by an oath to deliver up his two eyes" (i.e., the Sun and Moon). Thus was the name of the great god taken from him, and Isis, the lady of enchantments, said, "Depart, poison, go forth from Ra. O eye of Horus, go forth from the god, and shine outside his mouth. It is I who work, it is I who make to fall down upon the earth the vanquished poison; for the name of the great god hath been taken away from him. May Ra live! and may the poison die, may the poison die, and may Ra live!"

These are the words of Isis, the great goddess, the queen of the gods, who knew Ra by his own name.[1]

This famous story tells us that the goddess is already an adept but nevertheless feels there are limitations to her power. Therefore she is hungry for more knowledge and sets out to extort an important and revealing magical secret from her father the sun god. The technique is in part "tantrik", that is to say it manipulates the innate power of her own body and its secretions. She supplements this with a technique from the ancient lexicon of magic that remains in the repertoire of the practitioner to this day, albeit in modified form. This is a *diabole*, manipulating and torturing

---

1. The hieratic text of this story was published by Pleyte and Rossi, Le Papyrus de Turin, 1869-1876, pll. 31-77, and 131-138; a French translation of it was published by M. Lefébure, who first recognized the true character of the composition, in Aeg. Zeitschrift, 1883, p. 27ff; and a German translation by Wiedemann is in his collection of "Sonnensagen," Religion der alten Aegypter, Münster, 1890, p. 29 ff.

the sun god Ra until he reveals his secret name. It amply demonstrates the ambiguous side of Isis and arguably all Egyptian deities, who all have this capacity to use violence and deception to get their way.

Whilst on the topic of magick, it is worth noting that various pieces of knotted cloth strips were used as talismanic objects in the Isis cult. We should remind ourselves that the knotted cord is the hieroglyphic sign used to spell out the name of *Heka*, the god of magick. And even in Islamic times a magician was often referred to as "the blower of knots."

The pieces of cloth used in the cult seem to have began their existence as the garments worn by cult statues in temples. Temple cult mirrored daily life; for example the gods were *fed* and the rooms cleaned three times a day, just as in everyday life. This pattern is very similar to Hindu temple practice. Consequently the discarded clothes could be expected to retain some power called *sekhem* or *baraka*. Worn out garments were valued and so torn into strips as souvenirs for visiting pilgrims. It is likely that the "Isis bands" mentioned in several magical incantations are one and the same. The dividing of a whole garment into strips may also have given rise to the idea that they were some kind of veil. In actual fact Egyptian Isis does not wear a veil or headscarf. But in contemporary sources of classical times, when Egypt was ruled by the Greeks, the idea had become firmly established viz: Isis and other goddesses wore veils.

Another popular knotted amulet is the "blood of Isis" or the *Tuat* sign. It is also a strip of cloth, possibly a menstrual towel or tampon, used in magical medicine to aid women with such ailments. Over time the physical cloth is transformed into a piece of image magick, becoming an amulet carved in semi previous gemstone of the appropriate colour.

Tyet or Knot of Isis

In the final centuries before the common era Egypt was ruled by foreigners, the Persians, then the Greeks and finally the Romans. The cult of Isis continued to expand becoming popular throughout the colossal Roman empire. Isis became a universal goddess, assimilating other cults and spreading internationally via merchants, priests and private devotees. Osiris, her consort is repackaged as *Serapis* (Osiris+the Apis Bull), the focal point of a pantheon that included Anubis. Horus is also with her although he is more commonly known as *Harpocrates*.

Another feature of the mechanics of magick is also revealed during this period. This has to do with the relationship between a myth and ritual. The link was not obvious to us until we note how practical, magical spells are often prefaced by a mythological episode. Scholars call this a *historiola*. Essentially it is a short myth that tells you why the mechanical part of the spell works. The classical example is a magical object called a Horus Cippi. Cippi means small pillar. It is really a piece of sculpture, sometimes large and for public consumption, as in the so-called *Metternich Stele;* other times a small, domestic object. They invariably show the child Harpocrates surrounded by dangerous creatures such as the crocodile, scorpion or snake.[1]

The text inscribed on these objects tells the story of Isis hiding with her infant son Horus in the dangerous waterlands of the Egyptian delta. The person desiring protection from scorpion bites assumed the god-form of Horus, who is also stung but is saved from harm by this magick. These objects stood in basins which allowed the supplicant to drink the libations of water or beer after it had passed over the object and thereby absorbed the god-form of Harpocrates or Horus, to literally imbibe the power of his magick.

---

1.   Nora E Scott, "The Metternich Stela", *Metropolitan Museum of Art Bulletin*, nd.

Image of Horus Cippi, Metternich Stele

The Virtues of Isis

This is the time of the so-called Aretologies (list of virtues) or Doxologies (list of names). The *Aretology of Kyme* is the paradigmatic version. It originates in Memphis of the 2nd century BCE, but could be little earlier, a composition from the time of the first Ptolemies. Almost all these virtues have an Egyptian background although a few of them, as indicated with (G), are thus far only evidenced in Greek or Roman sources and thus likely to be an innovation of those times, with perhaps less or no real basis in earlier Egyptian culture:

1. [Lost]
2. [Lost]
3a I am Isis, the mistress of every land,
3b and I was taught by Hermes (Thoth) and with Hermes I devised letters, both the sacred (hieroglyphs) and the demotic, that all things might not be written with the same (letters).
4. I gave and ordained laws for men, which no one is able to change.
5. I am eldest daughter of Kronos (Egyptian = Geb).
6. I am wife and sister of King Osiris.
7. I am she who findeth fruit for men.
8. I am mother of King Horus.
9. I am she that riseth in the Dog Star.
10. I am she that is called goddess by women.
11. For me was the city of Bubastis built.

12. I divided the earth from the heaven.

13. I showed the paths of the stars.

14. I ordered the course of the Sun and the Moon.

15. I devised business in the sea.

16. I made strong the right.

17. I brought together woman and man.

18. I appointed to women to bring their infants to birth in the tenth month.

19. I ordained that parents should be loved by children.

20. I laid punishment on those disposed without natural affection toward their parents.

21. I made with my brother Osiris an end to the eating of men. (G) [1]

22. I revealed mysteries unto men. (G)[2]

23. I taught (men) to honour images of the god.

24. I consecrated the precincts of the gods.

25. I broke down the governments of tyrants. (G)

26. I made an end to murders.

---

1. Although thought to be a Greek innovation but there is a long standing tension in Egyptian cultures on this issue, which is an allegation levelled against to ancient Sethians. See *The Bull of Ombos* for fuller discussion of the background.

2. disputed by some authorities, in the earlier discussion of the Osiris myth, mysteries were mentioned in associations with his cult, which we might say is the classic location and ultimate origin of all subsequent mystery traditions.

27. I compelled women to be loved by men.

28. I made the right to be stronger than gold.

29. I ordained that the true should be thought.

30. I devised marriage contracts. (G)[1]

31. I assigned to Greeks and barbarians their languages.

32. I made the good and the bad to be distinguished by nature.

33. I ordained that nothing should be more fearful than an oath.

34. I have delivered the plotter of evil against others into the hands of the one against whom he plotted.

35. I established penalties for those who practice injustice.

36. I decreed mercy to suppliants.

37. I protect (or: honour) righteous guards.

38. With me the right prevails.

39. I am the Queen of rivers and winds and sea.

40. No one is held in honour without my knowing.

41. I am the Queen of war.

42. I am the Queen of the thunderbolt. (G)

43. I stir up the sea and I calm it.

44. I am in the rays of the sun.

45. I inspect the courses of the sun.

46. Whatever I please, this too shall come to pass.

---

1. Perhaps marriage was not such a formal thing in old Egypt.

47. With me everything is reasonable.

48. I set free those in bonds.

49. I am the Queen of seamanship.

50. I make the navigable unnavigable when I so decide.

51. I created walls of cities.

52. I am called the Lawgiver (Thesmophoros).

53. I brought up islands out of the depths into the light (G).

54. I am Lord of rainstorms.

55. I overcome Fate.

56. Fate hearkens to me.

57. Hail, O Egypt, that nourished me!

The Greek author must likely have modelled the above prayer on inscriptions from the famous temple of Isis at Philae in Upper Egypt. The temple was fully functioning within the same time frame. The architectural history of Philae begins in the 25ˢᵗ dynasty - but it was in the 26ᵗʰ *Saitic* period that it really became a significant part of Egypt's religious life. It was rebuilt during the reign of Ptolemy II (284-246BCE). Isis then replaced Hathor as the primary deity, made such by Nectanebo I of the 30ᵗʰ dynasty, grandfather of the last native king of Egypt, Nectanebo II.

There is a very fine collection of hymns to Isis from Philae. The following are examples taken from that collection either of which could be the source text accessed by later writers, either by reading it directly from the walls of the temple or from manuscript copies in the attached *House of Life*:[1]

Hymn VII

I play the sistrum before your beautiful face, Isis giver
of Life, residing in the Sacred Mound,
Eye of Re who has no equal in Heaven and on earth.

Great of love, mistress of women,
Who fills Heaven and earth with her beauty,
Divine mother of Kamutef,
Great Royal Spouse of Onnophris.

The August One, Great Lady in the Hall of the Prince,
The Mighty One in the Mansion of the sacred benben
stone,
One who moves freely in the barque of millions,
Who governs the divine barque.

Hymn IV

(Indeed), She is the Lady of Heaven,
Earth and the Netherworld,
Having brought them into existence through what her
heart conceived and her hands created,
She is the soul ("Bai") that is in every city,
Watching over her son Horus and her brother Osiris.

---

1.   Louis Zabkar, *Hymns to Isis in her Temple at Philae*
      (1988 : 107)

Apart from standard temple rites, Isis also benefited from a mystery cult of her own, something like the Eleusinian but with Egyptian antecedents. We noted earlier how the great "Hymn to Osiris" refers to a mystery cult operating in temples from at least the time of the New Kingdom if not before.

The mysteries of Isis would appeal to a Mediterranean world that was at the time engaged in the syncretization and reform of several older religious cults. So for example, viewing a god or goddess as some form of personal "saviour" was very much part of the spirit of the age. Isis was also the paradigm of loyal wife and mother but also promised immortality to her faithful devotees. Thus the last line of another aretology, that of Isidorus ends "Be merciful to me, relieve me from all pain."[1] This sentiment is thrown into stark contrast by the hymns from Philae, which invariably invoke blessings for the benefit of the king but nothing more personal.

The Classical Mystery Cult

A detailed account of the workings of the later mystery cults dedicated to Isis is recorded in Apuleius' Latin novel *The Golden Ass*. This story concerns Lucius who sets out on a quest to learn the secrets of magick but also to find sexual

---

1.   Zabkar (1988: 138)

love. He is tricked and cursed, being metamorphosed into an ass. The story is all about initiation and rebirth. The Ass in this period is very much viewed as an avatar of the god Seth, and therefore the enemy of Isis. The story is in turns hilarious, bawdy, tragic but then liberating. As mentioned above, when the goddess does appear it is as a saviour: hence in the "hymn" she says "I am here taking pity on your ills; I am here to give aid and solace".[1] The transformed Lucius becomes an initiate of the Iseum in whose vicinity he has been rescued. The novel's final chapter recounts in some detail the workings of the mystery cult into which he is inducted. Most expert commentators see this element of spiritual regeneration as the innovation made by Greek and Romans to an otherwise Egyptian tradition. Indeed traditional Egyptian temples may well have been modified or supplemented to accommodate this new cult activity.

Often overlooked, *The Golden Ass* could be classed as text of the Hermetic tradition. Other aspects of the mystery cult do have a clear Egyptian background, the most obvious being that it is Isis, who is the goddess into whose cult Lucius is initiated. The rhythm pattern used in the Greek texts is even said to replicate the shaking of the sistrum viz

---

1.   Gwyn-Griffiths *The Isis Book* (1975 : 77)

U – – UUUUUU where U is a short syllable and – long).[1]

Whilst Lucius is still in his lowly animal body he overhears the allegory of Cupid and Psyche, which is another tale of metamorphoses that Gwyn-Griffiths feels could well have originated in the Egyptian world. It is also a story that resonates with the Indian culture especially what we might call the *tantrik* tradition. It is a tale of Psyche's sexual awakening through her connection with Cupid, then their separation and continued yearning, itself a sentiment that can engender a transformation of consciousness.

Psyche embarks on a quest to find Cupid and this erotic feeling is a prelude to their union with god but also the achievement by both of immortality through commitment to sexual love. These are all important aspects of Hindu esoteric lore.

Meanwhile for Lucius, his liberation is about to occur in Cenchreae a place that in the ancient Greek world functioned as the harbour of Corinth. Here he experiences an epiphany, Isis appears to him in a dream, and she tells him to seek the annual procession at the beginning of the shipping season on the 5th of March. This is a form of the goddess adumbrated in very ancient Egypt, where Isis as patroness of boats, the

---

1.   Gwyn-Griffiths, *The Isis Book* (1975 : 348)

Forchner G (1988) Die Münzen der Römischen Kaiser in Alexandrien,
Frankfurt www.coinproject.com

sea and of navigation. Hence her name Isis *Pelagia*, "mistress of the sea", a popular form of the goddess at the time evidenced by the large numbers of Alexandrian coins which bear her image.[1] She is shown holding the situla, the breast shaped libation pot and the sistrum.

Ultimately this role in connection with navigation is one she took over from Hathor, whose head regularly adorned the prow of the sacred boat of Sokar, an ancient Underworld god and precursor of Osiris.

In *The Golden Ass* the liberation of Lucius from his asinine

1. RCC Fines "Isis and Pattini: the transmission of a religious Idea from Roman Egypt to India" *JRAS* 3.3.3.(1993) 377-391)

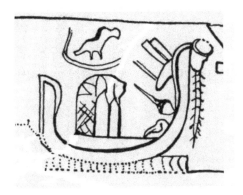

Sokar barque

disguise occurs at the blessing of a special boat in honour of the goddess. Here, at the head of this procession a priest holds a bouquet of roses, emblematic of Isis. Lucius is to eat those roses and this act will miraculously return him to human shape.

The magick of *The Golden Ass* is another feature that connects it to the Egyptian world-view. Hence here and in another work of Apuleius, *the Apology*, two kinds of magick are mentioned but with only an arbitrary distinction based on whether their instigator is Typhon ie Seth or Isis. The purpose in either instance would often be morally ambiguous. This is similar to the distinction made in early Christianity, where all pagan magick is "bad" by definition whilst Christian magick is "good".

In the story many important instructions and revelations come to the characters in dreams. Once again this view of the dream time as the theatre of magick is one with a long history best instantiated in the Egyptian tradition where the idea is first articulated.

Mystery Cults

The goddess Isis promises to end the cursed existence of Lucius who has been turned into an ass. The mechanics of his transformation, the eating of the roses, had been transmitted to him via the same dream discussed above. Given the despised status of the ass in ancient and indeed modern society, one must wonder how the creature will bring this off given the routine cruelty meted out to these lowly beasts of burden. Luckily Mithras the priest has been instructed via his dreams to let it happen. In another dream Lucius communes with the goddess who tells him his fate is to be initiated into her mystery cult. In "Pagan mystery cults ... the initiate is given a share in the fortunes of his or her deity, and by means of ritual dying and rising attains salvation".[1] In this the initiate is identified with Osiris, the husband of Isis. Her command to Lucius is that he should "enrol your name in this holy service, whose solemn oath you were asked to take not long ago, and vow yourself from this moment to the ministry of our religion. Accept of your own free will the yoke of service."[2]

1. Gwyn-Griffiths, *The Isis Book (Apuleius of Madauros,Metamorphoses, Bk XI)*, 1975 : 52

2. Op cit/ditto : 53

His religious vow is likened to a military oath, a feature of other mystery cults of the time. Interestingly one of the possible meanings of "Pagan" as used by early Christians is "civilian" ie one who has not enrolled in the army of the Jesus.

Initiation

The first initiation of Lucius follows several older Egyptian patterns. First he prepares with a ten day fast or dietary restriction. Egyptian weeks were also divided into ten days. His initiation begins on the evening of the final day, a symbolic death during the hours of the night. He begins with a ritual purification or lustration. These rites were staged in a special underground crypt beneath the Iseum. Here there is also some kind of arrangement for the pre-initiation baptism and lustration. In Egyptian temples there were sacred lakes for the same purpose.

With the *uninitiated* "far removed", the candidate assumes the posture of Osiris, not in a coffin but on a special ritual bed, perhaps modelled on that used to re-assemble Osiris after his dismemberment by Seth. The culmination occurs nominally in the sixth hour of the night with a vision of the sun-god in the Underworld. This is also the moment in Egyptian religion when the sun god was remade anew each day.

We can assume that the candidate was in a deep hypnotic sleep; according to Plutarch this was induced by burning special incense he calls *Kyphi*. It could also be induced by the administration of a mild narcotic such as the Egyptian Blue Lily (*nymphaea caerulea*) known to influence dreams and widely used in Egyptian and indeed later Hindu esoteric rites. All of this is entirely in accord with the schema set out in ancient Egyptian books of the afterlife such as *The Book of Gates*. At dawn the candidate is reborn with the sun.

Egyptian temples of all periods often do contain special crypts but this is much more obviously so in those temples built during the late period under the patronage of the Greek and after them the Romans. At Thebes in Upper Egypt one finds a collection of local temples that have been so adapted. At Karnak, an entire suite of rooms, the so-called Opet, was attached to the temple of Khonsu, complete with several crypts. A few miles further south is the temple of Isis at Deir el Shelwit to be discussed below. There is another ruined temple in the Valley of the Queens, a small temple possibly dedicated to Thoth in Habu village, nowadays known as Qasr el-Aguz (lit. the castle of the old lady) and a large temple of Hathor close to the pharaonic worker's village of Deir el Medina. There was even one lost local shrine connected with Seth, although thus far only a few small relics of this have been found. All of these are part of a late classical mystery cult and are suggestive of a ritual

Images of the Ptolemaic Opet shrine attached to the Temple of Khonsu at Karnak, shows it looking north, the pylon of the Khonsu temple just visible. photographed by the author.

sequence of rites connecting all these shrines. The best preserved of these at Karnak had its own dedicated entrance gate cut through the Temenos wall, facilitating activities set apart from those of the main temple campus.

Initiation visualized

As an exercise in "experimental archaeology" here is an imaginative reconstruction of the candidate's journey culminating with initiation into the mystery cult. The setting are the already mentioned complex of small temples in ancient Thebes in Upper Egypt. Your first initiation will be into the cult of Isis. For some weeks you have been living in special accommodation in the small Roman town that surrounds the temples of Isis at Deir el Shelwit. You exercise by walking to the nearby cultivated fields and beside the irrigation canals and lakes.

West of the town, beyond the fields, begins the desert where people only venture to bury their dead in the mountain necropolis. The desert is the domain of dangerous animals, wild dogs and wolves who howl in the night. Although there are well trodden paths across the desert, your mentor advises you to beware of some of the creatures who have no inhibition against attacking a person when they are alone or defenceless. Beyond the low desert, mountainous cliffs rise up to form the Libyan plateau.

You cast your mind back over the period leading up to your initiation. As the fateful day approaches the rhythm has changed. You now spend the best part of your time reading sacred books in the temple, sometimes discussing an obscure point with a mentor known as Hierogrammatos. He is a scribe in the service of the temple, a priest who interprets sacred texts for you and guides you through the process of initiation. Mostly you meditate in the quiet rooms set aside for this within the temple proper. You make a point of only eating simple food, which invariably means vegetarian, nothing to

Special entrance connecting the Opet to the Khonsu temple (left) at Kharnak

over stimulate the senses. You have also cut down on wine, preferring to drink pure water sometimes prepared with a calming cordial made by boiling hibiscus herb and allowing it to cool to a delicious sustaining drink. Everything is designed to calm the senses and to avoid nourishing negative thoughts. Some say these thoughts are like daemons that should not be fed.

Your mentor has already recommended that you pay special attention to *The Book of Gates*. You know it almost by heart and find it comforting. You feel it will be your guide in the transition to the new life that awaits you.

You mull over the events of what will soon be your old life. You think about the chain of causes that has led you to this moment and about the new life to come. It is a period of incubation, almost as if you will give birth to a new you, it reminds you of how the philosopher Socrates spoke of himself as the *midwife* of knowledge. The Egyptian way of reckoning things says there are ten days in every week. They also say that ten months is the period of time a mother incubates a baby in her womb.[1] In your meditation each day of the ten corresponds to one of those ten months; so as each day progresses, you become ever more mature and ready for rebirth.

Other things your mentor told you that once seemed obscure and required much thought, now begin to make sense. He asked you to make a decision about the emblems to be present at your place of sleeping on the last night. He made you think about the design of the beds in the temple sleeping chambers. They all have four legs, but these are carved to resemble those of particular animals. The head-

---

1. Egyptians began the count from 1 rather than 0, hence 10 rather than 9 months.

Inside the Opet are many corridors and several crypts. On the left can
be seen many pilgrims gouge marks, evidence of personal piety.

boards have been individually carved with one of three animals. You surmise that it is one of these animals that will carry you over to the otherside during your night journey. Those animals are the fearsome hippo, the cow with the sun suspended between its horns, and the leopard. All three are rich in symbolism. It dawns on you that your mentor is asking you to consider the nature of each of those beasts as it relates to your transformation. In what sense are you like a hippo, cow or leopard? The hippo does not eat meat but is extremely fearsome, especially when protecting its territory or young, the cow is a symbol of Isis herself, powerful but also nurturing. The leopard is a carnivore whose form represents pure, naked power.

The fateful evening arrives, the eve of the New Moon. You bath in the temple baptistry, a brick lined sacred lake east of the temple. You change into a simple full length robe of natural, undyed cloth. Your mentor leads you to the special chamber in which is a comfortable couch in the form of your chosen animal. On it is a mattress of folded linen. There is a small table, upon which there are two small terracotta jugs; one filled with water, the other contains a mysterious substance which your mentor tells you to drink, promising that it will be pleasant and help you through the night. This done you settle down on the couch. Your mentor reads the familiar lines that open *The Book of Gates*:

Painted reliefs in the Opet depict special mythological scenes. One of the most enigmatic in all , Osiris been visited by a night bird complete with phallus.

As your mentor reads, you drift into the world of sleep and dreams:

"You who came into being from Re,
from his Glorious Eye.
Granted to you is a hidden seat in the Desert.
Come together all those created by the Gods.
The God has taken your measure in the Necropolis.
As he does for all those living on this Earth;
created as it is, from his right eye, the Sun.

The desert is bright,

I give it light,

With what is in me.

Souls of the West, those who would destroy humanity,

my glorious Eye is on you.

I have ordered the destruction,

destruction of the enemies of Ra;

of the enemies of those upon the Earth,

where the chosen ones are.

Breath be given to you, among whom I am

Let there be rays for you,

dweller in the region of offerings.

To you is restored the diadem in the desert.

To you is restored the diadem in the necropolis.

The Gods shall say:

"Your presence is commanded by the great God,

He who lifts up his arms and moves his legs; as shall you,

Come to us, you who share his essence; and say

Hail to the One in His disk,

Great God with numerous forms."

The Egyptians divided the period between sundown and sunrise into twelve equal parts called hours. Although you sleep through this whole time, you are roused at the beginning of each hour by the sound of a priest reading the appropriate section from *The Book of Gates*. Each of its twelve chapters corresponds to each of the hours. You are momentarily

excited by those words before again lapsing into sleep. Your dreams keep pace with the lines as you rest, half heard and half remembered. In those hours you dream of entities and your soul's journey from dusk to dawn. In the silence it is as if you are watching a drama at the theatre or observing the progress of a night pageant. Sometimes you are one of the actors in the drama:

"*1ˢᵗ Gate*

At the first gate, a large serpent stands
His name guardian of the desert is upon the door.
He opens for Ra, and those upon the Earth,
Full with the chosen ones of the Gods.
Your mind as a God speaks,

from the prow of the sun-boat

Saying to the wise serpent: Guardian of the Desert"
You hear lines concerning the star goddess and you recall
how you've been taught that she is also a form of the
goddess Isis, your patron. In the morning you rise, reborn:

"On the sun boat of the morning, lifted by the Abyss
Abysmal waters surging up, from the faraway world.
Kephra the sacred scarab,
As new sun born through the eastern mountains
Isis and Nephthys bearing him up,
to the waiting Goddess of the sky.
Who stands above this earthly sphere,
out of the old and into the new,
You are lifted into her arms,
Mother of the Gods, Nuit."[1]

You wake refreshed and renewed. Details of your visions
during the night journey are for you. One ancient initiate
commented on the whole experience thus:

"I approached the boundary of death and tread on

---

1.   Based on Alexandre Piankoff (1974) *Egyptian religious texts
and representations*, 6 vols, Bollingen 1974. The complete
rendition is published in Rodgers & Maskell, *Contemporary
Western Book Of The Dead*, 2012 : 168sq

Proserpine's threshold, I was carried through all the elements after which I returned. At midnight I saw the sun flashing with bright effulgence, I approached close to the gods above and below and worshipped them face to face". [1]

In *The Golden Ass*, the ancient hero Lucius does not remain in the temple but resumes his normal life. He moves to Rome where he takes up residence in the Iseum Campensis and after a further gestation period of nine months is offered a second initiation on the winter solstice. A third initiation swiftly follows. In all Lucius is initiated as priest of Isis, then priest of Osiris, then of Isis & Osiris together.

1.   Gwyn Griffiths, *The Isis Book (Apuleius of Madauros, Metamorphoses Bk XI)* 1975 : 99

Isis in Thebes (Deir el Shelwit)

Much of the above reconstruction is based on my explorations of one of the last shrines to Isis built and dedicated in Egypt. Deir el Shelwit is just a few miles south of Luxor on the west bank of the Nile. This whole area is one of the world's largest archaeological sites, a vast treasure house of pharaonic temples. It made me wonder why there was any need to build yet another temple. These later buildings are often overlooked but in my opinion they present us with evidence of a big religious change because they seem to combine traditional temple rites with a mystery cult.

Deir el Shelwit from south, shows back wall of sanctuary with feature for external offering on western face.

At *Deir el Medina*, home of the famous village of pharaonic craftsmen, a small Ptolemaic temple is dedicated to the goddess Hathor. A few miles away is *Deir el Roumi* in the valley of Queens, are the remains of another such monument, they are so fragmentary, the original dedication remains unknown. A stone's throw from Medinet Habu is *Kasr el Aguum* which means "Castle of Old Woman" which was sacred to Thoth. As we already know, *Deir El Shelwit* featured Isis. Across the Nile is a fascinating extension to the Temple of Khonsu at Karnak, known as the Opet - although this is not currently open to the public.

Nowadays these distinctive and related shrines bear the modern Arabic prefix "Deir" which means monastery. Monasticism is itself an eastern innovation whose origins are usually ascribed to Buddhism. The re-tasking of these temples as monasteries is the work of Egypt's Coptic Christians. Perhaps there was already something in the way they were used before that made them particularly suitable for meditation and initiation. After all, Christianity was itself a mystery cult than grew within this same milieu.

The road to Deir el Shelwit goes south from the *Memnon* ticket office, passing the front of the temple of Medinet Habu and through the modern village of Habu. Passing through its winding streets one is soon in the desert. For several miles the dirt track passes through the traces of a

city, abandoned in the very remote past. This is Amenhotep III's royal colony of Malqata. There is a long ridge east of the track, which was mistakenly labelled as a Roman hippodrome by Napoleon's mapmakers. In fact, it is the remains of a long harbour wall that once held back a vast artificial lake, 1½ miles long and ¾ mile wide!

Deir el Shelwit was built when Egypt was ruled by the Romans and is thus one of the last constructions of the Egyptian religion. It was discovered in the 19th century but then largely ignored and only recently has it been fully renovated and opened to the public.

Published sources about it can be difficult to obtain and only available in French or Japanese! Basically there is one Holy of Holies. These days Deir el Shelwit gets very few visitors. As is common at most smaller shrines, if you ask the guard, he will leave you alone for some quiet meditation. I explored the pro-pylon, the formal entrance to the sacred precinct. The causeway leads past a sacred lake in which priests and initiates would have purified themselves before ritual. Looking west beyond the mud-brick temenos one can see miles of empty desert. In meditation the desert represents the other world. The central shrine is a riot of images and mythological scenes which would have kept the adepts well occupied. The neophyte would naturally begin by studying the western wall which has four main tableaux, sandwiched between two strips of hieroglyphs showing the dedication and additional information about the contents of each scene. Those above scene 155 read:

"(This is) ISIS, the great, the mother of God, the eye of Ra, who resides in the mountains of the West, the great

Deir el Shelwit, view west from the remains of the propylon
to the sanctuary

stellar womb that takes the "Sun God" and the stars from evening to the morning. Who makes a sarcophagus into which Ra descends along with his stars, so he can get to his place each day, after he has illuminated the Underworld and traversed the Kingdom of the Dead. Where those in the afterlife gave praise, when (his) rays merge with the body of Osiris ("the heart of mats") and the disks are combined in one disc, and after its shinning appearance as a child in the morning, rests in the arms of the two claimants (ISIS and Nephthys), going into the horizon after its (heavenly) crossing in the night bark, enormous in its power, whose great name is Monthu of Hermonthis so that Apophis is felled by (his) fire." [1]

The above is precisely the journey that the candidate takes in his nocturnal initiation.

The frieze at the bottom shows a procession of the Nile god Hapi bringing the riches of all the regions or nomes along the Nile. Isis is prominent in all of the main scenes, often together with the other deities with whom she has an longstanding connection. For instance Isis shares the temple with Monthu - an primeval warrior god with strong local connections. Remember that the Isis shrine at Deir el Shelwit is located between Armant, *Hermonthis* of the Greeks,

---

1. (After D Kurth's translation in *Einführung im Ptolemäische, Eine Grammatike mit Zeichenliste und Übunggsstücken*, I, Hützel, 2007, p563-564)

or "land of Monthu" and Thebes, stronghold of Amun-Min. Monthu's other cult centre is at Madumud on the east bank just a few miles north of Karnak. So perhaps this otherwise obscure pairing with Isis is inevitable given their proximity. Other inscriptions in the shrine tell us more about Isis & Monthu. The gods addresses her as *Tanent* - the primordial Earth Mother. All of this may help us understand how Isis interacts with other gods as she travels. When we follow in her footsteps to India, Isis is paired with a south Indian god called Murugan - the spear bearer!

In scene 155 at top left of the wall, the Roman emperor Hadrian is shown in adoration before the goddess Isis. To the modern eye the image is rather obscured by blocks of text. These are exactly like the speech bubbles one finds on graphic novels and record the words, in this case hymns to Isis.

The great block of hieroglyphs, ten lines, in the centre of the picture is actually a lovely hymn to the goddess. In it she takes on the attributes of several older, sky goddesses, principally Nuit. Apart from its beauty, this hymn also captures precisely the way Isis assimilated the mythology of older goddesses. The preponderance of astronomical imagery is taken more or less word for word from the liturgy of the

---

1.   An arrangement of this text is published in *Phi-Neter: power of the Egyptian Gods.*(2014 :)

sky goddess Nuit. *The Dramatic text of Nuit.*[1] is the source of this story of her eating her own piglets. The Hymn at Deir el Shelwit reads something like:

"Praise you ISIS! Hail you, you magic oak,

mistress of the two lands, rejoice!

Hail to your Ka, hail your Majesty,

great ISIS, mother of the gods

The disk it hymns you, it sings to you ("in your womb");

Atum praises you "in your body" at night.

Because you are the sky, inside which the Sun travels, in whose region find the shining Moon and the star in the sky!

The mouths of the horizon pay homage to you, because you are the mother sow who eats her piglets and gives birth to them everyday.

In the sektet boat rising, allowing the affairs of the two truths to reside in the mandjet boat

Ra rises Because of you in the early morning

and Atum sets in the night

The immortal Star: who offered the Southern sky it praises you

Because you're the Lady of new year Satis (sothis).

Mistress whose light is at the side of the Orion

Left: Internal Noas or shrine with ambulatory space all around. Detail: Nile god Hapi from Kom Ombo. Author's photo

Inside Deir el Shelwit. The four most important scenes on the west wall are conventionally numbered from bottom left as 152, bottom right 153, top left 154 and top right 155. Photo: Ayman

The imperishable Star Gods of the northern sky, elevate you

The circle of the gods resting in the necropolis, are satisfied, because you are the great IPET, the guard of the Big Dipper (Seth)

The cave dwellers in their lairs rejoice for you, because you are Hathor, the Princess of the westerners

These which are sleeping on their bellies choose you, (for) the images on their standards

The two truths in the Hall of two truths,

because you are the truth about which the two truths are

By your saying what is what in duat, you live! [1]

The two scenes in the lower register differ. The leftmost scene (DC152) shows Hadrian offering Maat to a double image of Monthu. And in scene to the right (DC153) he offers Maat to another pairing of gods, Amun-Min and Monthu-Re. Monthu is a falcon or bull headed warrior god representing the scorching power of the sun but also, when the black faced, white bull *Bacha*, the raging fury of battle.

We are fortunate to have the Deir el Shelwit so well preserved, especially the carvings on the interior of the *naos*. the layout also gives some clue as to the mechanics of cult worship. There is a "corridor of the mysteries" that surrounds the inner shrine and must have allowed adepts to circumambulate as well as gain access to the private rooms used for initiations and rites not suitable for the "profane" i.e. uninitiated. In one of these rooms on the northern side is a place of purification, a *webit* which has a type of crypt commonly found in religious buildings of this time. If you think again of the initiation of Lucius, it seems likely the crypt was the place in which the candidate experienced the

---

1.   A von Lieven (2006) "Der Isishymnus Deir Chelouit 154. 1-10" *AcAnt* (B) 46 2006 p165-171)

hours of the night in hypnotic sleep, rising at dawn with the sun, renewed in body and soul.

The Indian example to be discussed below has both a secret chamber and corridor. All of these late period edifices show evidence of the evolution of Egyptian religion into the syncretic, mystery cults that proliferate at the beginning of the New Age. The cult of Isis assimilated older elements and developed innovative religious activity. In its design we get a precise snapshot of the work of the "Hierogrammatos" - the scribe at the service of the temple, a priest who interpreted sacred texts and would be mentor to the neophyte.

Shore Temple at Mahabalapuram, Tamil Nadu

The transfer of Isis from Middle East to South Asia

Before discussing the Isis & Osiris story in connection with India, there are several other Near Eastern myths that are sometimes considered possible sources of the Pattini myth. Oberesekere favours Syrian mythology over the Egyptian. There is indeed a proven Syrian connection with South India. And this influence is reciprocal, as confirmed by recent research of Professor Diarmaid MacCulloch who concludes that monasticism in the Near East owes its existence to the influence of South Asian Buddhism. [1]

On the other hand, Kerala in South India has an enclave of Syrian *Christians*, whose foundation narrative begins with the apostle Thomas. Indeed Syrian Christianity is still one of South India's important denominations. Thomas is supposed to have founded his first church at Kotunkolur. His hagiography tells of a conversion of Brahmins, who one must remember would not have been a major group in what was then Buddhist & Jaina territory. Some authorities argue that this is all 'back story', that developed to explain the

---

1.   Diarmaid MacCulloch, *Silence: a Christian History*, London, 2013

antiquity of the Syrian church in India. Nevertheless, it remains entirely possible that St Thomas was popular amongst an established colony of Syrian traders.

Adonis

The Syrian myth of Adonis is sometime seen as another example of a god who dies and then resurrected, albeit temporarily, by the actions of his lover Aphrodite. The most detailed and literary version of the story of Adonis is a late one, and is found in Book X of Ovid's Latin, ie Roman *Metamorphoses*.

In its Greek telling, Aphrodite falls in love with the beautiful youth Adonis who then gets himself killed by a wild boar, said to have been sent by Artemis. Like many Greek deities, she is capable of jealousy, in this instance because of the hero Adonis' hunting skills! In some versions of the myth, it is Artemis' revenge against Aphrodite for instigating the death of Hippolytus, her favourite. Yet another version blames the god Ares, who is jealous of Aphrodite's love for Adonis. Apollo also has a grudge and wants to punish Aphrodite for blinding his son, Erymanthus.[1]

---

1.   https://en.wikipedia.org/wiki/Adonis

Aphrodite rushes to the wounded Adonis, alerted to his plight by his dying groans, he dies in her arms. She mixes his blood with nectar then sprinkles it on the ground from which springs the beautiful but short-lived flowering anemone.

Attis

Another mythic migrant into India is the cult of Attis and Cybele. Attis is the offspring of the daemon Addistis, abandoned at birth but then nurtured by a he-goat. As Attis grew, his long-haired beauty was godlike, and Agdistis [his real mother] also called Cybele falls in love with him. The foster parents of Attis sent him to Pessinos to wed the king's daughter. According to one version of the myth, the King of Pessinos was Midas, the man with the golden touch. Just as the marriage-song was being sung, Agdistis/Cybele appears in her powerful transcendent form, and Attis is driven mad and cuts off his own genitals. Attis' father-in-law-to-be, the king who was giving his daughter in marriage, follows suit, prefiguring the self-castrating *corybantes* who devote themselves to Cybele. Agdistis/Cybele later repented and saw to it that the body of Attis would never decay.[1]

---

1.   https://en.wikipedia.org/wiki/Attis

All of the above myths have some iteration in South India. Even so, it is still really the story of Isis & Osiris that seems the closest fit to the original mythology of the temple of Kotunkolur in Kerala. Northern India may have received some of this story via a different source, transmitted along the land route via Afghanistan, the backdrop to Alexander the Great's famous conquest and establishment of a Bactrian-Greek monarchy.

South India also had its own direct connection with the Near East via the captains and crew of merchant ships.

2000 years ago, the cult of Isis had reached the Hellenistic form as described above. The goddess of the Egyptians was still perfectly recognizable beneath the Greek innovations. It is this synthesis of Egyptian & Greek cult that we should expect to find in the Indian setting. This does not rule out the possibility of finding additional strata of meaning that had found their way to India during an earlier era.

Communication between South Asia and the Middle East is evident even before Greek & Roman times. For example, the Bronze Age Indus Valley culture, which flourished from about 3300-1300BCE traded with Egypt. [1]

---

1. Wendy Doniger, *The Hindus: an alternative history.* Oxford University Press. 2010 : 67.

There was an even earlier infusion of astrological and astronomical lore from the Babylonian world. So for example, it is well known that Indian and Greek astrology are very similar. Every one of these layers of ideas survive in India, overlaid or mixed with native technology.[1]

An interesting example of the iconography of Isis survives in the personification of the zodiacal sign Virgo. It is no longer easy to recognise the goddess Isis in modern representations. However in the rare Sanskrit astrological text the *YavanajAtaka* (literally "the Greek Story"), Virgo is described as a goddess holding a torch while standing on a boat. This is precisely the same as Isis Pelagia "mistress of seafarers" or Isis Pharia, "protectress of the Pharos harbour" where once stood one of the wonders of the ancient world, the lighthouse of Pharos, the ultimate guide for seafarers. [2]

Earlier we traced the cult of Isis from its beginnings at a time of the building of the pyramids, and perhaps even before that. We followed the goddess as she transformed from a

---

1.   D. Pingree: "History of Mathematical Astronomy in India", *Dictionary of Scientific Biography*, Vol. 15 (1978), pp. 533–633 (533, 554f.)

2.   Richard Fynes p386 quoting D Pingree (1963) pp 225ff.of Sphutjidhvaja AD 269

Image of Virgo from an Egyptian sarcophagus of late classical period.

local deity to the focus of the first national religion in human history. Knowledge of her travelled beyond Egypt to become the nucleus of the first global religion with temples as far flung as South India and North to the Roman trading station on the banks of the Thames in London. Isis was for all that, a player in what became the most famous religious drama of all time, the story of the holy family of Osiris, Nephthys and Seth.

In the beginning, she was a subordinate to her husband Osiris. The paradigm of the loyal wife was destined to always remain an important aspect of her cult. But there was also internecine conflict and jealous rage between the two brothers, Osiris and Seth. Like Biblical Cain, Seth kills then dismembers Osiris. After this, Seth tries to hide his crime by scattering and concealing the body parts of his slain brother.

In the drama, Isis discovers her magical prowess whilst searching for and eventually finding the body of her dead husband. Isis revives Osiris, perhaps the archetypal and earliest version of the myth of the dying and resurrecting god.

But the reward of her work does not last, the resurrection of Osiris is a temporary respite, just enough time for the couple to engender a magical son who will eventually grow, protected by his mother, to avenge his father and take his rightful role on the throne of Egypt.

Richard Fynes suggests,[1] that Indians would have recognized

---

1. Richard Fynes : "Isis and Pattini: The Transmission of a Religious Idea from Roman Egypt to India", *JRAS* Series 3.3.3. 1993 : 383

the Egyptian myth, as an example of their own belief in the power derived from suffering; the lamentation of Isis for Osiris is echoed in the Indian goddess Pattini's overwhelming grief for her husband Palanga. Isis and Pattini are both archetypal *mater dolorosa*.

This is what Joseph Campbell calls a *monomyth*, a perennial story that has entered into the web of almost all of the current batch of great world religions. From these simple beginnings as consort to the god Osiris, Isis accumulates more and more powers. By Hellenistic times, when her cult first reaches Indian, the list of these powers is so extensive it comprises a long hymn or doxology, as in the example on page 62.

In the examples noted earlier, we encounter Isis as patroness of seafarers. Isis as a goddess of the sea is something more often associated with Hathor, whose cult Isis assimilated in the past whilst still exclusively an Egyptian goddess. This characteristic is one that becomes much more prominent in the era of the great maritime empires of the Greeks and their Roman successors.

Pattini, when human was Jaina

Jainism, is still practiced by many millions of devotees, making it one of the world's oldest religions. In the 6th century before the common era, its founder Mahavira, a contemporary of the Buddha and one of its most influential teachers, began his mission. Some even say that venerable Mahavira was a reformer of Jainism rather than its founder. Thus the origins of the religion may be far older.

Its three main principles are: non-violence, relativism, ie things are only true from a particular point of view, and non-possessiveness. Because buying, selling, and banking do not involve physical violence they are today very popular livelihoods for Jain householders, ie those not following a monastic or ascetic lifestyle. In the Indian version of the Isis & Osiris myth, the corresponding characters Pattini and Palanga are said to be of a Jaina merchant family, and one that has significant connections to maritime trade. The pluralism and open mindedness of Jainism, might be one of those factors, that made it easier for Egyptian religious ideas to find a foothold in India.

The Temple of Isis in India

India is of course famous for its wonderful stone temples, artistic masterpieces of the ancient world. The history of stone architecture in India begins really at the same time as Buddhism. One of the very earliest stone monuments would be the famous Barabar caves, built under the patronage of Buddhist Emperor Ashoka of the Mauryan dynasty (c322 - 185BCE). His renowned tolerance and generosity, a reformation after a previous life of great violence, is demonstrated by this gift of habitation cells to a non-Buddhist sect of Ajivikas. The carving of the Lomas Rishi cave shown in the picture, is actually a copy of a wooden original but made entirely of stone. This celebrated cave is so famous that it is the destination of the characters on that fateful daytrip in E M Forster's *A Passage to India*.

It is often argued, that Buddhism required a new kind of building to accommodate its adherents in a communal setting. This made it possible for the monks to teach other monks, or preach to the laity. Early Hinduism and other religions had no such requirement. The history of Indian architecture begins with these highly decorated caves, which perhaps originally functioned as winter sanctuaries for a small number of otherwise peripatetic monks.

There is another kind of mysterious building known from this time whose relationship to the story may be significant. Apart from these communal rooms described above, there

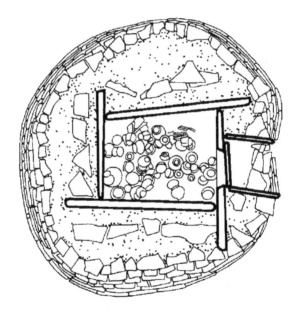

Mortimer Wheeler, My Archaeological Mission to India and Pakistan, Thames & Hudson 1976. *The photographs of the Cyst burial at Brahmagiri, Arcot are from his book. The layout of the stone walls anticipate the offset doors of later Buddhist stupas.*

Wheeler made the first major publication of the Roman presence in India, the big discovery of his day.

is another very characteristic Buddhist building, known as a 'stupa', that forms the nexus of many Buddhist sacred spaces.

The literal meaning of 'stupa' is 'burial mound'. The design of these is very elaborate, with much symbolism in the decoration combined with a *geomantic* representation of the entire Buddhist cosmology. The feature I wanted in particular to draw your attention to is this hybridization of two functions, temple and tomb. The fact that Buddhist stupas combine tomb and temple is *conceptually* very similar to the Egyptian approach to religious architecture. The most obvious parallel being the famous pyramid tombs which are also some kind of temple.

Buddhist burial practice is also in marked contrast to orthodox Hindu, where there are major taboos concerning the dead. Modern Hindus invariably cremate their dead, and as far away from a temple as possible. Any orthodox Hindu would find it hard to countenance a combined temple and burial space, even if it were purely symbolic.

Or so it seems. In fact, even in Hinduism, it is possible to find ancient examples of burials rather than cremations. It is said that a modern Indian citizen who desired burial rather than cremation, could appeal to this precedent. This is not speculation, some, admittedly not many, contemporary Hindus have made such claims. The evidence they point to

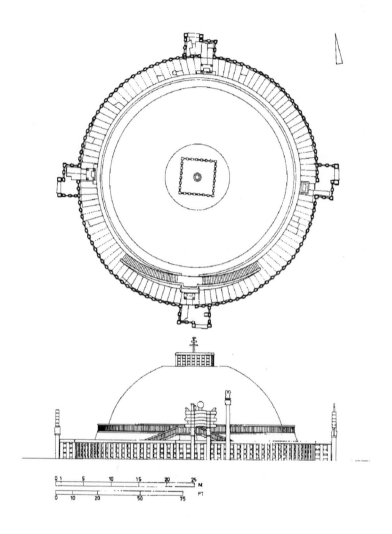

Buddhist stupa from : Andreas Volwahsen, *Living Architecture: India*,
Macdonald 1969. Note the offset gateways which make the groundplan
a swastika

Megalithic tomb from Vengupattu

Below: Lomas Rishi Cave, Wiki Commons

is widely scattered throughout the South of India, in the form of a large number of megalithic burial sites, dolmens and cyst burials. These structures, although they resemble similar dolmens of the European Stone Age are in fact Iron Age, built sometime between 1000BCE and the time of Christ (see picture).

These megalithic structures are always built on high ground near important water management resources such as canals, dams and reservoirs. It is extremely likely that the people honoured in these structures, were in some way responsible for the dissemination of the knowledge of irrigation that transformed Indian agriculture at this time. This is another point of contact between South India and ancient Egypt where Isis, the consort of Osiris, is also linked with the control of the Nile, the river that some say 'built' Egypt:

"I make the navigable unnavigable when I so decide."
The Aretology of Kyme, vs 50

Another curious fact about these seemingly 'anachronistic' Stone-Age, megalithic structures, is that they are the groundplan used in the already mentioned Buddhist stupas, and tomb-temples. This fact jumps out at you when you compare the ground plan which is a swastika. Because of the perversion of religious symbols wrought by the Nazis, it must be repeated that the swastika is a benign symbol, a Sanskrit word approximating in meaning to auspiciousness.

These sources flow through the entire spectrum of religious architecture in India, which reached its apogee in the famous South Indian style. Although Buddhists were the pioneers of stone religious buildings in India, the Hindus soon found their own uses for the Buddhist models. From these beginnings, the Hindu temple developed its own independent style.

The ancient historian Pliny recalls that the Romans also built a temple at Musiris. The precise lineaments of this temple are to be discussed below. There is no reason to doubt that this temple could also have included a shrine for Isis, patronised by the colony of traders.

Tabula Peutingeriana

The piece of evidence for the existence of a Roman temple at Musiris that I want now to look at, is rather extraordinary. It is said that a picture is worth a thousand words. And in point of fact a picture of a classical temple situated in Musiris in south India does exist. It comes from an ancient Roman map known as the *Tabula Peutingeriana*.[1] This beautiful artefact is a scroll seven metres in length. It was crafted in

---

1. Annalina Levi and Mario Levi. *Itineraria picta: Contributo allo studio della Tabula Peutingeriana* (Rome: Bretschneider) 1967. Includes the best easily available reproduction of the Tabula Peutingeriana, at 2:3 scale.

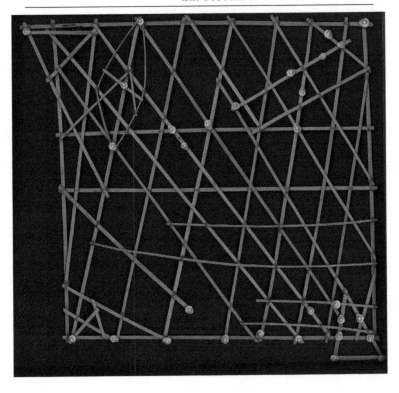

Native sailing map, Micronesia, split cane and shells, Pitt-Rivers
Museum 1897.1.23. These maps are much prized and difficult to come
by, they successfully show island location, ocean currents, waves and
swell.

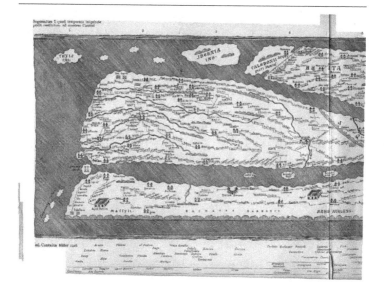

Tabula Peutingeriana #1

the fourth century of our era but was undoubtedly based on much older sources.

The map is not the territory

Judged by the cartographic conventions of our own times, and based on accurate surveys and satellite imagery, this map may initially look very inaccurate. But in truth, all maps are somewhat of an illusion, in the sense that they are attempts to represent in two dimensional form the three dimensions of our mundane world. These facts should be borne in mind when judging the cartography of an older time. Our own map projections may seem reassuringly safe,

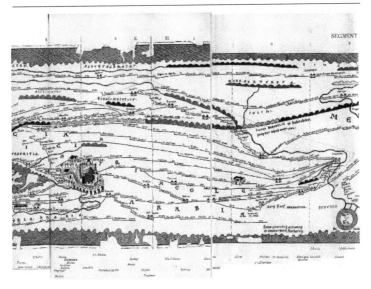

Tabula Peutingeriana #2

but they are as much founded in conventions as the older forms.

So for example, even a knotted rope can function as a useful map given knowledge of the conventions used in its construction. Take for example, a string with three knots, A B & C. The divisions between the knots could represent the relative distances between the three ports, thus B to C is twice the distance of A to B. If A to B were equal to the daily run (dromoi) of a sailing vessel, then the journey from B to C will take twice as long.

The *Tabula Peutingeriana* map is a detailed *schematic*

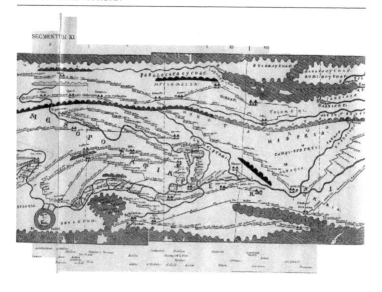

Tabula Peutingeriana #3

representation of the then known world. Papyrus technology of the time determined that it must be drawn on one continuous narrow strip, just over 1 foot wide and 22 foot long. The whole could then be rolled and safely stored. The method of manufacture determined the mapping process. Put simply, all areas, have to be shown schematically in one narrow strip. Only when these conventions are understood can the value of the Tabula be fully grasped. In a sense the Tabula is rather like the modern tube map of the London Underground. Because it had to be printed as a large oblong poster, it does not represent an actual bird's eye view of London. It is a schematic based on the relative positions of the stations. As well as major place names, the unknown

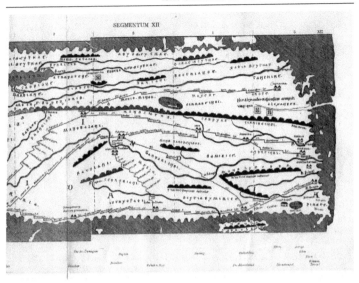

Tabula Peutingeriana #4

Roman cartographer shows major roads. The importance of a site is reflected in the relative size or detail of the pictogram used. Thus Rome is shown as a very large feature. This element should be held in mind when below we use the Tabula to hunt for a temple in India.

TP#1 above shows a transcription of the first, and most damaged section of the scroll. It represents the extreme west of the Roman World. If you look carefully, you can see ancient Britain as a lozenge shaped island, with at its northern end Caledonii (Scotland). All this is in the top right quarter of the section. Just left or west of it you can see the mythical island of Thyle or Thule. The main section of the map that resembles a whale's head with gaping mouth, is Spain (Galicia). In the "mouth" of the whale you should be able to just make out the twin pillars of Hercules ie modern Gibraltar. The lower jaw of the whale represents North Africa.

So if this is the west of the Roman World, by moving to the end of the scroll we should find the Far East. The bottom right section is India. The Indian map shows a temple in what must be the region of *Musiris* in South India, the location for our quest for Isis in India. On the next page is the Indian section close up and in detail above in which you should be able to read in the stylized temple the words; "Templi Augusti." - the temple of Augustus, the Roman emperor (63BCE - 14CE).

Nowadays, few believe in 'the glory that was Rome'; such a thought has become politically incorrect. Ancient Rome is seen as at best a poor second to the much more refined culture of Greece. Some modern people feel an empathy for the cultures conquered *by* the Roman empire. Although embattled Rome's rise to power was by no means inevitable, some find much to admire in the records of Rome's vanquished European rivals. Some wish to draw our attention to the Roman's own ambiguity concerning the value of their ancient culture: Horace, the greatest of all Roman poets, wrote that 'Captive Greece captured the

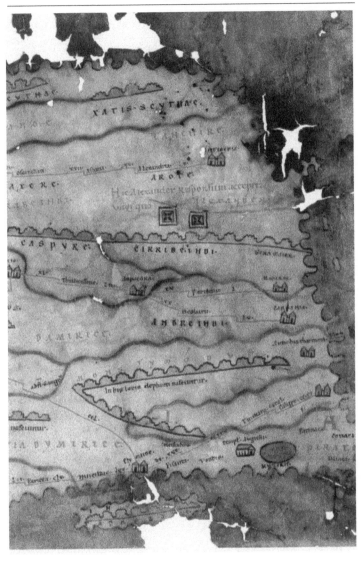

Tabula Peutingeriana (detail showing India)

victor and brought the arts to rustic Latium.' [1]

All this is called 'what if' historical speculation. I don't feel any need to take sides in some long lost struggle. Personally I find many things to admire in Roman culture, even its art and literature. There are also many things to repel the modern mind. But nothing I have seen undermines the fact that Rome was one of the three great civilizations of the Mediterranean. And whatever my personal preference, Rome plays a large part in our strange story. We have to know something about her, if we are to make sense of what we find in Egypt and India.

India was never a part of the Roman Empire, which makes the presence of a Roman Imperial temple all the more remarkable. It was almost certainly built by the permanent merchant colony of Romans and Greeks, whose existence we know of from several reliable sources. It is my contention that the Roman temple on the map must have some connection to the later Hindu temple of Isis/Pattini built nearby, perhaps even on the same plot.

This important Hindu institution at Kotunkolur is reputed to be constructed upon the foundations of something older, so why not the Roman original. As discussed elsewhere this still active Hindu temple has a 'secret chamber' of old

---

1. Horace, *Epodes* 2.1.156

masonry which could well be Roman in origin. We have to know more about this building, as it is extremely likely that it had an some influence on other religious constructions in the area.

Temples & Rituals in the Roman World

Scholars say that in religious matters the Romans were conservative. This does not mean there were no religious innovations or changes in religious life over its long history; far from it. But alongside new religious trends they preserved and indeed privileged forms of orthodox worship modelled on those of an ancient Etruscan past.

The Etruscans were for many centuries the most important early rivals or perhaps counterparts of the Romans in the Italian peninsula. They lived in small cities but they idealized a simple rural life based around a compact family unit. Their tombs are decorated with pastoral scenes of life after death in which the family relived their time together at a perpetual banquet. The soul of the recently dead was ferried to these Elysian fields on the back of a white horse. Rituals for the living took place in a special enclosure on high ground known as a *templum*, from which the Latin term temple is derived.[1]

---

1. Aldo Massa, *The World of the Etruscans* (New York 1973 : 95)

A system of divination (Latin: *Disciplina*) was carefully preserved and utilized by the Romans via various handbooks. It might therefore be theorized that the grand religious buildings of the Romans were not the true focus of their faith. For this, we must look to the Etruscan cult. Central to this was the use of augury, a religious technology transferred, almost lock, stock and barrel to the Roman world during the period when the 'Etruscan' king Tarquin ruled Rome. During that time, a great temple was built on the Capitoline hill dedicated to what was to become the three principal Roman deities - Jupiter, Juno and Minerva.

Before this, in about 700BCE, the Etruscans adopted the Greek alphabet and along with it several Greek religious ideas. Of secondary importance to the 'templum' was some kind of sanctuary for the pantheon of Etruscan gods. No Etruscan temple has survived, all that is known comes from the Roman architect Vitruvius' description at the time of Augustus.

The Etruscan sanctuary was almost square with pillars at the front entrance. This shape and various parts were determined, irrespective of any artistic considerations, by rigorous and inflexible religious rules that included astronomical observations. It must always have two separate rooms. One was situated at the back and formed the rear of the temple (*postica*). It almost always comprised a triple *cella* or naos. This was not a subterranean space, but a windowless room enclosed on three sides by a thick wall in which were set statues of deities.[1]

The front half (*antica*) was a portico with several rows of pillars, into which the three chambers of the cella opened. A Greek temple was built from top to bottom in stone. Greek temples were usually ringed by steps but the ancient Romans and their Etruscan precursors favoured a single approach from the East. The Etruscan built almost entirely in wood; only the pillars were sometimes made of stone.[2] This preference for wood was not because the Etruscans lacked skill as stonemasons; far from it. They chose to build their sanctuaries in wood, just as they used terracotta for statues and canopic caskets, because these materials had a special religious significance.

In this building, cult offerings were made to the Etruscan pantheon. But the real heart of the religion remained always in the *templum* enclosure in front of the shrine. It was here,

---

1. Leonard Schmitz in *Smith, Dictionary of Greek and Roman Antiquities* 1849 | 2d ed. improved and enlarged | Boston, hereafter referred to simply as *Templum*)

2. Aldo Massa, *The World of the Etruscans* (New York 1973 : 95sq

that the Etruscans practised their elaborate system of augury or divination. Scholars say that 'inner revelation had no part in Tuscan divination, which was completely inductive, concerned solely with the interpretation of external signs.'[1] There is still something quite logical about the Etruscan method of divination. The Etruscan augur initiated a divination by planting his staff on some eminent, auspicious ground outside of the city or pre-existing *templum* (*pomoerium*). From this central *gnomon,* the dome of space was divided into an array of lines radiating out from the four cardinal directions, then further subdivided into the either eight or sixteen segments. If an astrological template was to be used, then the space was divided into twelve equal segments.

The Roman historian Livy called the Etruscans a religious nation *par excellence* and the Christian writer Arnobius says that Etruria is the mother of superstition.[2] There was hardly any aspect of Etruscan life that was not touched by their

1. A Massa, *The World of the Etruscans* (New York 1973 : 4. See also Cicero 'De Divinatione' & Sybille Haynes, *Etruscan Civilization: a cultural history* (BM Press 2000). Illustrated section on divination at pp278-281.

2. Titus Livius (Livy) *History of Rome,* Vol I Book 5.1 Everyman's Library, Translated by Canon Roberts, J. M. Dent & Sons, Ltd., London, 1905. Christian father Arnobius, *Adversus Nationes,* vii, 26-27.

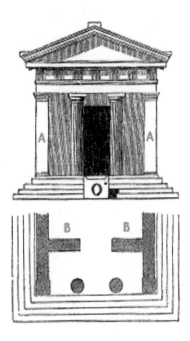

Engraving from Hirt's *Geshichte der Baukunst* (reproduced from *Templum*). A-A = antika, B - B The cella or naos

advanced use of omens, a science they claimed to have learnt from the Chaldeans. Even the layout of a city was structured according to a scaled up *templum*, with activities in each segment that were thought appropriate for that area. Etruscan *Templum* or template was probably derived from Greek *Temenos*. Similar examples of sacred geomancy are to be found in almost every society and is well known in south Asia.

When the augur (*haruspicina*) has defined or circumscribed
the place where observations were to be made, a special tent
was erected (*Tabernaculum capere*) also known as the *templus
minus*. The top section of the augur's staff functioned as a
sighting device through which, the specialist could
concentrate on the corresponding section of the sky or
heavens, also known as the templum, from whence a sign or
omen was expected to appear. Three varieties of omens
were contemplated. Perhaps, the earliest and most common
concerned the phenomenon of lightning strikes, so called
thunderbolts, which might also include meteorites. The
source within the celestial templum was interpreted both in
terms of its divine origin and its destination. An ancient
handbook for interpreting such signs was then consulted to
finish the omen. This same technique was also applied to
the observation of birds (*auspicium*). There are accounts of
the augur observing a particular resting bird, waiting anxiously
for it to fly away and thus fulfil the omen.

The third most common and arguably least attractive method
was the examination of animal or occasional human entrails
after sacrifice. Here we see the entrails framed by the real
and notional template in various ways. The most favoured
organ for this kind of divination was the animal's liver,
which was divided along the lines of the terrestrial template.
The organ was then minutely examined by a specialist and
certain features and oddities interpreted and the *omina*

sought in one of the ancient handbooks. This kind of divination is very ancient craft known of all over the known world. The techniques were not unique to the Etruscans.[1]

It is unlikely that divinatory systems are somehow built into the nature of reality. They are almost always 'conventions', arbitrary methods of mapping symbolic space. But there again, I would remind you of my comments earlier concerning the nature of maps. The map is not the territory, even so if its conventions are consistently applied, the map, or divinatory schema, will, over time, generate reliable results.

The Romans in India would have found some of the same techniques widely in use. It would be interesting to see how much similarity there is between the Indian and Roman/Etruscan versions of the omen books. The Etruscan books of interpretation are ultimately derived from Babylonian versions.[1] It may be difficult to argue that this was all transferred to India by the Roman colonists, as this kind of divination is the common currency of the ancient world. India received its own independent transmission of Babylonian astrological and divinatory lore at a much earlier date.[2]

1. Koch, Ulla Susanne, (2000) Babylonian Liver Omens. Univ of Copenhagen Press
2. D. Pingree: "History of Mathematical Astronomy in India", Dictionary of Scientific Biography, Vol. 15 (1978), pp. 533–633 (533, 554f.)

From the Indian and indeed Egyptian point of view, any of the above practices would be familiar. For example, and as we shall see later on, a bird omen, not dissimilar to the Etruscan variety, plays an important part in the Myths of Isis in India, ie the Pattini Cycle. The layout of the former Pattini temple at Kotunkolur follows principles comparable to the Etruscan *templum*. Furthermore, the idea of the geomantic city plan based on a ritual template is a commonplace of the Indian world view. To quote one example, the goddess Pattini in her travels in search of her dead consort, enters the city of Madurai via the east and exits via the western doorway. We will discuss more of this below.

The fall of the Greek city of Syracuse to forces of the Roman Republic in 214BCE further opened Rome up to the culture of the East with Greece acting as the bridge between East and West. It is said that before this time, the Romans knew little of exquisite or fine things.[1] As they came into contact with others they demonstrated a natural propensity to synthesize any religious or intellectual ideas they encountered. Cicero brought Greek philosophy to the Roman Republic and in the process coined a number of new Latin terms to deal with the subject matter e.g. Humanism, which

---

1.   Charles Freeman, *Egypt, Greece and Rome: Civilizations of the Ancient Mediterranean* (OUP 1996)

the Greeks later borrowed back as 'humanismos'.

Probably the most famous, and also arguably least understood aspect of later Roman religion was the hero cult of the emperor. It is to this aspect of Roman religion that we must now focus.

In the earliest phases of development there appear to have been very few temples in Rome. Places of worship were mostly basic altars or shrines of the kind already described. Roman temples of later times were constructed in a Greek style. The little drawing of the Temple to Augustus in Musiris shown on the map of India, is by Roman standards, very simple in design. It likely had two columns at the front, so called *In Antis*, ie two columns between or incorporated into the posts or pillars (*antae*) flanking the doorway. Vitruvius, our main Roman guide on temple design, says that 'The length of a temple must be twice its width'.[1] The drawing conforms to these measurements having four columns on the long side. This rectangle would be divided by internal walls into a *pronous* and the Holy of Holies or *cella*. This cella would be square. Ideally, the statue in the cella would be set in the east, facing the western entrance in such a way, that the eyes of worshippers would fall upon

1. *The Architecture of Vitruvius Pollio,* Book 4 2.

it as they walked in. If there were more than one cult statue, these would be incorporated into prominent niches.

"The cults of the Roman emperor performed by the Greek cities of Asia Minor during the first three centuries of the common era confound our expectations about the relationship between religion, politics and power. The civilized, complex cities, with their ideals of autonomy and freedom, had to accept subjugation to an authority which, while not so alien as to make adjustment impossible, were external to the traditional structures of the city. The answer to the problem lay in finding a place for the ruler within the framework of traditional cults of the gods."[1]

The Temple of Augustus on the Palatine in Rome must have been, as one might expect, an enormous structure, with eight columns across a frontage of 32 metres. Its vaulted roof, if such it was, would have been the highest in Antiquity at 150 feet. The large cella would contain, in various niches, statues of Augustus, probably his wife Livia and perhaps other deified emperors. Behind this was a smaller shrine to Minerva, one of the three principal deities of Roman religion. Although egress into this temple was possible from the back

---

1.　S. R. F Price, *Rituals and Power: the Roman imperial cult in Asia Minor* (1984 : 155)

of the Augustan shrine room, the temple of Minerva had its own major entrance and indeed orientation. This is a good illustration of a point made by Price.[1] It was not common for the emperor to share his temple with a traditional god and where he did, there was some sort of subordination to the resident deity, this relationship was expressed in the architectural arrangements.

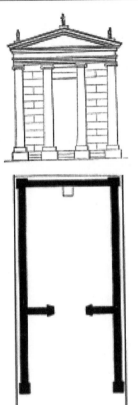

Small imperial temples in the 'colonies' would have been based on these traditional models but in scaled down form. Their small size gave very little scope for biographical or narrative relief about the emperor. This kind of thing would be confined to the freeze of the altar, which stood near the cult statue.

The cult of the Roman emperor invites a comparison with

---

1.   S. R. F Price, *op cit* (1984 : 2)

the Egyptian cult of divine Kingship. This ancient practice is characteristic of the cult of Osiris; the earthly king becoming, post mortem, an avatar of this god in the Otherworld. The Roman practice sits easily alongside the Egyptian. The temple of Isis at Deir el Shelwit discussed earlier, was commission-ed by the Emperor Hadrian whose image appears in several of the carvings.

The drawing shows the front elevation and plan of a simple Roman or Greek style temple. The equivalent *cella* in the contemporary Hindu temple of Kurumba Bhagavathy Devi in India is a mere 30 feet square, ie much smaller than even the most modest Roman or Greek equivalent. If we assume for a moment that the existing Karumba Devi temple was built over the foundations of a Roman *cella*, then the external portico conforms with Vitruvian rules of proportion.

Were there subterranean structures in Roman temples? Yes indeed there are several examples of this, such as in the three tier structure at Cyzicus in the Balikezir region of modern Turkey. This had an upper level, and a ground floor connecting by a maze of tunnels to a basement.[1]

There are also cases where the Roman cella was not accessible to any human being, and coincidentally various

---

1.   S. R. F Price, *Rituals and Power: the Roman imperial cult in Asia Minor,* (1984 : 155)

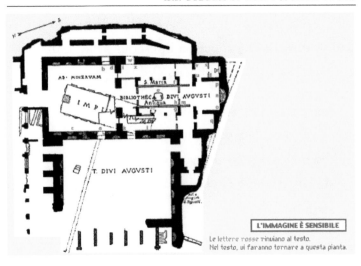

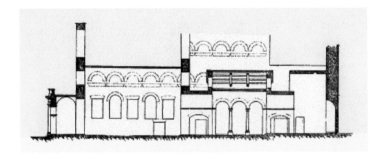

Temple at Cyzicus in the Balikezir region of modern Turkey This
temple had an upper level, and a ground floor connecting by a maze of
tunnels to a basement.

stories related to calamities that had befallen persons who had ventured to cross such a threshold. One of the most famous comes from Sophocles *Oedipus*.

> Out on it, lady! why should one regard
> The Pythian hearth or birds that scream i' the air?
> Did they not point at me as doomed to slay
> My father? but he's dead and in his grave
> - *Oedipus Rex*

Rome in India

The above discussion leads us to the possibility that the remains of a Roman temple might still be visible somewhere in south India. No such structure has yet been found in situ, although there is a Hindu temple in the right area which is sufficiently old that it might conceivable have incorporated some Roman masonry into its foundations. This is the still functioning Hindu temple at Kurumba Bhagavathy Devi. Its location is at Kodungallur or Kotunkolur also known as Cranganore near modern Cochin, the capital of Kerala.

Karumba Devi is another name of the goddess Bhagavati, a form of Kali. Recent research indicates that it may have had several earlier dedications, including one to Pattini, a goddess or spiritual entity these days only worshipped in Sri Lanka, where she is the guardian goddess, much as Isis was *Agathadaimon* of Alexandria in Egypt. The remains of her cult were then assimilated to either Kali or Draupadi. Her exile from Kerala is explained by the shifting fortunes of the rival kingdoms of this region, the Cholas, Pandyas and Chera, the later whose name lives on in the modern state of Kerala.

The wars between Hindus and Buddhists also changed the religious map. Although they once co-existed quite peacefully, by the time of Christ violent inter-communal disputes were the norm. And during the Indian late Middle Ages, ie from 13th-18th centuries, Buddhism suffered a terminal decline in the land of its birth and many former Buddhist structures had been re-dedicated or destroyed.

Some say Pattini got her name from 'Patni' meaning wife, because the archetypal, dutiful wife was one of her most obvious attributes. This is one of many characteristics she shares with Isis, her Egyptian antecedent. The eminent Indian anthropologist Gananath Obeyesekere points out that she is also often called "a Pattini", and thus can be considered as one of a special class of female supernatural entities. She is also called Kannaki, which was her birth name before she assumed her divine form, a process described at length in the myth (see below).

It is widely accepted that the Indian port of Musiris, which was famous in Classical times, must have been close to the what is now the Kotunkolur temple. The precise location of Musiris has probably been erased by the periodic shifts in the floodplain of the mighty Periyar river. In ancient times, Musiris was the first landing point for vessels plying the 'Hippalos' trade route mentioned earlier. The Cochin area is still home to several 'alien' religious communities.

The Karumba Devi temple is built in the Malayalam style,

not as famous as others but well worth exploring here in detail.

Malayalam is an architectural style unique to Kerala. The aesthetic is surprisingly modern, with long, steep gabled roofs; very functional for this west coast, which receives the full force of the annual monsoon storms. It also strongly resembles Roman tiled roofing! Could this be another example of Roman and Classical influence?

An aerial view reveals the ancient principles of construction and the underlying structure. It is based on a perfect square with the Holy of Holies, and the copper plated *kovil*, in the

Kotunkolur temple today

centre. This kovil has a regular square footprint and its steeply pitched roof forms a perfect, if diminutive pyramid! Nearby is a Shiva temple built in the 12th century. It is advantage to us, in that we can view the geomantic principles much more clearly, because it has fewer *ad hoc* accretions that obscure the basic outline. Rather surprisingly, the scale of this is much the same as those small satellite pyramids built for Egyptian queens at Giza

The same four-square arrangement is just discernible for the older Kali Bhagavati temple. Ancient architectural manuals from India say this square footprint is a stylized man, seen front on in a crossed legged posture.

This remarkable saga was opened up in the 1970s when a local Brahmin called Induchudan was commissioned to write a history of his temple and he called it *The Secret Chamber.*[1]

This intriguing title is a reference to a continuing mystery connected to the temple's construction. There is a door on the western wall of the sanctum sanctorum of the Kali shrine which opens to give a view of the western wall of the secret chamber. There are no doors or windows above ground, the walls are made of granite with stone roof. On

---

1. Induchudan, V.T., *The Secret Chamber: a historical anthropological and philosophical study of the Kodungallur Temple,* [Trichur: Cochin Devasan Board.] (1969 : 2)

Karumba Bhagavati Temple at Kotunkalur, view from East

Kali festival days, this door is opened to allow certain 'VIPs' to see a red cloth draped over the secret chamber.[1] There is no way into this chamber from inside the temple. Something terrible and mysterious is presumed to be located in the secret chamber, but nobody knows what. Even so the existence of the chamber and connecting tunnel have an impact on the life of the temple.[2]

As in some classical Near Eastern temples, there is a taboo

1. Induchudan *The Secret Chamber* (1969 : 13)
2. *Ditto*

Above: Shringa Puram Mahadeva temple, Cochin (Google earth)

Below: The Giza-pyramids and Giza Necropolis, Egypt, wikicommons

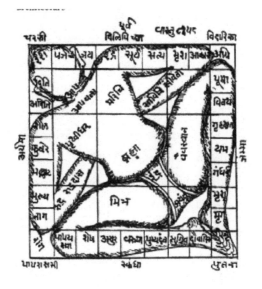

Image of man superimposed, with navel/omphalos/womb at centre.
From Andreas Volwahsen *Living Architecture - Indian* (London 1969)

about looking into this room. According to local tradition,
a carpenter engaged in doing repairs on the roof glanced into
the chamber and lost his sight! A long passage leads from
this chamber in eastern direction, travelling 100 yards to the
outside.[1] The mouth of this passage was sealed 100 years
ago due to health and safety concerns. The tunnel is said to
be infested with snakes, a fearsome form of the goddess in
both Hinduism and Egyptian religion. The chamber lies to
the west, with the passageway running from the west to the
east.

1.　　Induchudan *The Secret Chamber* (1969 : 13)

Two houses called *Kunnah madhom* and *Neelath madhom* stand guard over the entrance. The people who live in these houses are called Atikals. In the past, especially within the Jaina religion, Atikal meant 'saint'. Today Atikals are a caste of so-called 'degraded' Brahmins, who play no formal part in the rituals of Karumba Bhagavati temple, but who nevertheless are the formal owners and act as administrators and secular management. Could it be that the Atikals are the descendants of the original owners of this temple? And what of the secret chamber, the passageway and the countless unorthodox practices associated with this temple. Could it be true, as some say, that the 'remains' of Pattini, a goddess whose rites closely resemble those of Egyptian Isis, are hidden in this chamber?

The distinguished anthropologist Gunanath Obeyesekere pours cold water on such a suggestion, but there is only really one way to find out. His theory about the chamber is hardly less unusual. He thinks that the chamber was used for initiations. He has in mind classical Near Eastern mystery cults in which, a neophyte was reborn as a "female" priest or acolyte. This "female" status was signalled by special dress code, principally the wearing of the veil, or in some cases genital augmentation or even castration. India

Aerial view of Karumba Devi temple today (Google earth)

is known for its cult of Hijras, transsexual devotees of the goddess, seen by some as a continuation of the Near Eastern cult of Attis, whose devotees performed the cruel rite of self castration.

There is also a possible theme of castration discernible in the myth of Osiris. Osiris is castrated by his brother Seth. In Indian myth, a similar fate befalls Pattini's unfortunate husband Palanga. However, as I described in some detail above, what we know of the classical initiation rites, specifically those into the cult of Isis, do not involve the

Ground
Plan

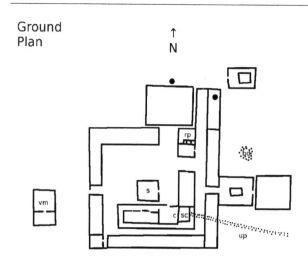

Key:

sc	=	secret chamber
s	=	kovil/central shrine
up	=	underground passage
k	=	Kali shrine, image faces north
c	=	crimson cloth
sml	=	7 mothers
s	=	shiva, faces east
rp	=	sickle sword
bd	=	offering made in Bharani fest
vm	=	Vasurimala
dp	=	special door

candidate in such a drastic act as castration, neither did it involve permanent celibacy.

For Obeyesekere the squat secret chamber is both tomb and womb, the tunnel is present for the process of symbolic rebirth. The tunnel's west-east orientation is highly suggestive of the journey from sunset in the west to birth at dawn. The candidate spent the intervening hours in the Underworld.

Obeyesekere investigated whether similar 'initiation' tunnels might exist in other local temples. He found another rare example in the temple to Shri Rama in Tiruvilvamamala. At this site he learnt that devotees passed through the tunnel in a rite called *punarjani*, literally "rebirth". This spiritual process could be related to Tantrism in which initiation also plays an important role, and thus could make uses of this otherwise mysterious architectural feature.[1] What we in the West call "Tantra" can itself be seen as a late classical religious tradition, one that develops or re-emerges, depending on your point of view, in the early centuries of the common era. That is to say, the rise of Tantrism and the heyday of the Pattini cult share the same time frame. Moreover, Tantrism can be shown to exhibit elements from an international esoteric tradition, and may itself be influenced by Near & Middle Eastern religious movements such as Hermeticism or Mystery cults.[1] Either way, temples

---

1.   Obeyesekere 1984 : 538

in the region could, according to Obeyesekere, show traces of some sort of initiation cult in Kerala.

Who is Pattini?

"Traditions of the [Pattini-Palanga] ... myth have deeply permeated South Indian culture, often to be transformed into something totally different."[2] Our quest for Isis in India leads us to her door. It will take us amongst spirit mediums and folk magick practitioners. In the end, her cult will merge with that of the dominant mother goddess of Kerala, who is now Bhagavati Kali, although scratch beneath the surface of the Kali myth and one finds Pattini.

Scholarly opinion in Sri Lanka and South India is that Pattini is a Hindu goddess, whose cult originated in the south, but was then transferred to Sri Lanka by a Keralan King called Centtuvan, who was a Hindu. In this reading of events, he established a shrine to the goddess in old Vanci, present day Kotunkolur. He is said to have dedicated this shrine as a response to a series of events and natural disasters. All of this as recorded in the *Shilappattikaram*, the *Tale of the Anklet*.

An alternative theory is that it was as a goddess of the Jaina religion that she influenced the celebrated Tamil story,

---

1. Obeyesekere 1984 : 539
2. Obeyesekere 1984 : 540

which has become the region's venerable epic and the inspiration for many popular songs and ritual dramas. It soon spawned a sequel called the *Manimekalai*, which tells the story of the daughter of the beautiful Madhavi, with whom the husband of Pattini has a passionate but ultimately financially ruinous affair. Mamimekalai eventually become a Buddhist convert.

Others say that Pattini is a goddess common to Jainism and Buddhism but also an amalgam of other obscure traditions such as the heterodox "ajivika" theology. Ajivaka - literally "lifeless beings" are an extinct religious group whose philosophy is only known from accounts in rival Buddhist and Jaina sources. They practiced extreme aestheticism and were fatalists in the sense that they believed one could never escape fate.

It was Induchudam, the Brahmanical author of the history of *The Secret Chamber*, who first suggested that there were traces of the goddess Pattini hidden within the modern temple. His view was based initially on the proximity of the old city of Vanci, the seat of the ancient kings of Kerala (Cera). This has been now definitely identified by scholars as modern Kotunkolur. Records say that King Centtuvan installed an image of the goddess Pattini somewhere in his capital.

The carving shown in the picture overleaf is of a still *in situ* stone pillar in the old part of the temple. It shows a woman wearing a distinctive headdress of a kind not currently worn by Hindu women and is uncommon even on images of Hindu goddesses such as Kali. In fact, Pattini is the only 'veiled' goddess in Indian iconography. These days her cult is confined to Sri Lanka, an area that in the past did have important connections to Kerala. Anthropologists concur that her cult must have migrated from Kerala to Sri Lanka.

In Singhalese ritual Pattini is wearing a veil such as that shown in the carving. This veil is a *Mottakkili*. A garment or shawl, similar to this, appears in 19th century Singhalese paintings of women. It is also worn by priests performing rituals for her cult such as the "blessings of the anklet". In this rite, the cross-dressing priest, his shawl held in place with "tiara" like broach, uses a symbolic anklet jewel to bless pilgrims.

In Sri Lankan rites the priest sometimes wears seven such veils when impersonating the goddess. There we have it, the Dance of the Seven Veils springs to mind from the Near Eastern cult of the goddess Inanna. This number is highly symbolic in Near Eastern religion and to be fair equally so in South Asia. Seven is one of those special numbers, whose power probably derives from primordial stellar lore, ie the constellation Ursa Major or perhaps the sevenfold Pleiades.

In the Pattini cycle it is the god Shakra, the Buddhist version of Indra, who begins by accosting her but then compensates for his aggression by giving her seven veils. The *Mottakkili* veil mentioned above is one of those gifts from Indra. This veil and the anklet are crucial sacred symbols even though they do not correspond to the way women actually dress in everyday Shri Lanka society, today or indeed in the past.[1]

Another parallel we have to consider is the headdress worn by Muslim women. Veils were a rare feature of Indian dress and iconography before the Moghul period, and the large influx of Islam. Even so it is unlikely that Islam was the origin of Pattini's veil. The Pattini cult well predates the Muslim conquest of Indian. It is more likely that her veil is part of the original cult. Pattini wears such a garment in Shri Lankan Buddhist and Hindu myth and this association is confirmed by the old stone carving in Kotunkolur temple.

Some have even suggested that Pattini's veil owes something to the symbolism of the Catholic Virgin Mary. But this merely indicated yet more evidence of Near Eastern origins, where veils are associated with the mother goddess.

The Kali-Bhagavati temple at Kotunkolur received its current dedication in the 14th century of the common era. This is some centuries after the radical reform of Hinduism wrought by Adi Shankara Acharya (788-820CE). He was

---

1.   Obeyesekere 1984 : 539

Image carved on ancient stone pillar in Kotunkolur temple shows
veiled woman.

born in Cranganore, the anglicised form of Kotunkolur. Is this mere coincidence or perhaps there is something special about this place? Some scholars say he was originally a Buddhist, and from this, drew his inspiration for the new form of Hinduism called Advaita Vedanta. He promulgated this new doctrine by a campaign of preaching & debating, backed up by a monastic organization modelled on Buddhist brotherhood (*Sangha*).

Advaita Vedanta is itself a doctrine with many similarities to Buddhist theology. In the next few centuries, Buddhism & Jainism disappeared from the region, indeed the whole of India; although their influence lived on.

Bhagavathi that is usually translated as "goddess", could also be from *Bhaga* which means vagina! From this we might see the goddess as one who understands all the mysteries of life. In the temple, she takes a more defined form called Bhadrakali, a popular, ferocious avatar of the goddess, with three eyes, and multiple arms, standing on the prostrate body of the demon Darukan, who she has defeated and decapitated. According to one popular account "she likes blood, red silk and red flowers. She has fangs and smallpox pustules, rides on a ghost, wears skulls and snakes and is loved as a benevolent mother. She is a pot, a curved sword and a mirror. She lives in the temple, the rice fields and in the sacred groves. In various rituals and spontaneously,

women and men go into trances and communicate her
wishes, allowing her to continually change." [1]

Her image in the Holy of Holies at Kotunkolur is six foot
high, carved from the wood of the jackfruit tree. With
multiple arms she holds weapons given to her by six gods,
unable to defeat the demon, who has tricked them previously
into promising that no man would kill him. In her hands she
holds the severed head, a palm leaf text, a trident and a
sickle sword. She may also hold (it is difficult to tell) a bell,
a serpent, an anklet and a vessel of some kind.

This distinctively shaped sword carried by Kali is known as
a *Ram Dao*, a ritual chopper used in decapitation of sacrificial
animals. It has several similarities with the ancient Egyptian
Khopesh, the standard battle sword of the army of the
pharaoh.

The temple at Kotunkolur has on display a colossal version
of this sword. It is assumed this is a ceremonial version of
the *Ram Dao*, it being too large for actual use. Could it be an
heirloom from a time when the temple had closer relations
with the Middle East?

The Egyptians saw in the constellation *Ursa Major* the shape

---

1. Dianne Jenett "Red Rice for Bhagavati 1998 *ReVision*,
    Winter 1998 v20 i3p 7

Image of Pattini from Singalese Temple
(courtesy of Professor Geoffrey Samuel)

of this sword, the Kapesh (*Kps*). According to their stellar lore, every god had a corresponding constellation. The very earliest sources tell us that Ursa Major was the constellation of the god Seth, the murderer of Osiris. Thus in astronomy one often finds the origin of ancient myth, the entire cyclical movement of the constellations re-enacting the passion of Isis & Osiris.

In Tantrism Bhadra-Kali is also one of *matrikas* or divine mothers. Usually said to be ten in number, but in a special shrine at Kotunkolur they are seven! These mothers, also known as the *mahavidyas* meaning "great knowledge", each of them instantiates a particular kind of wisdom. Again, I draw your attention to the coded repetition of the sacred number seven within the mythology of this temple.

Unlike other regions of India, in Kerala, Kali is viewed as an auspicious and benign goddess. This difference in understanding is another indication that she is may be a local goddess who has only a superficial association with Kali, perhaps only assimilated to the Kali cult at some late historical juncture.

Today, the Kali puja practiced at the temple differs from what is normal elsewhere in Kerala. The oldest local form of Kali worship is called *Sanghakali*. The *Sangha* is familiar to us as the name of the Buddhist order but must therefore signify "army" or "brotherhood". *Sanghakali* is one of the oldest forms of the art of ritual drama in Kerala. Also known as *Yathrakali*, it emerged in the sixth century of our era and at a time when the south of India was predominantly Buddhist. It is an art form of the sect known as *Namboodiris*, who are Hindus but whose name literally means "new Buddhists".

The Namboodiris were migrants to the south whose appearance coincided with the end of Buddhism in India. These priests represented the dominance or hegemony of the Aryan cultural group over the indigenous Tamils and Dravidians. Their association with the military is reflected in the name of the ritual form, *Sanghakali*.

The complicated Sanghakali ritual form has a number of elements comprising ritual drama, martial arts, chanting of hymns and cult acts. At Kotunkolur there is no practice of drum rituals *(kanamirikkal, aarkal, paana)* which normally accompanied cult acts such as the planting of sacred trees for example *alstonia scholaris*.

In its stead, pilgrims visit the temple in March and sing obscene songs and perform obscene acts and gestures, directed at the goddess. This occurs at the festival *Bharani* which is an asterism based on the astronomical observations in the month of Kumpan (Feb-Mar). This would also be a time of thanksgiving to the goddess for "opening of the ways". An example of one of these, here quoted from

Contemporary lithograph or "God photo" of Kali from Kotunkolur

Obeyesekere, more than demonstrates that the label obscene
is no exaggeration:

> "If you want to fuck the goddess of Kotunkolur
> you must have a penis the size of a palmyra tree." [1]

Pilgrims who visit the shrine refer to the goddess as
Orramulacci, which means "single breasted one". However,
the statue of the goddess Kali currently installed in the Holy
of Holies is not single breasted! As we shall see, Pattini, not
Kali, is the only goddess in the Indian tradition said to be
single breasted. In the myth cycle she brutally tears off one
of her breasts in a rage. This is another indication that she
was in fact the original goddess of the shrine, which still
bears her name.

As discussed earlier, the priests in overall charge of the
temple are known as *Atikals.* Studies show them to be
descendants of Brahmins, although they have these days lost
many of their religious privileges. This loss of status means
they are said to be degraded. Ironically, some explain this as
due to their affiliation with Bhadra-Kali and rites that
involved the use of alcohol. They do, however, still have
some liturgical functions, although the details of their rites
remain a closely guarded secret. They are in effect a secret

---

1.   Obeyesekere (1984: 481)

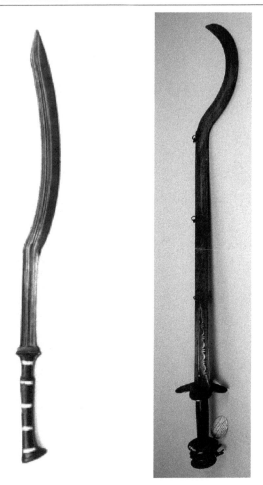

Left: Tutankhamamun's sword, found in his tomb in the Valley of
the Kings, Photograph by Harry Burton, ' Copyright: Griffith
Institute,
University of Oxford'.

Right: Ceremonial sword called a Nandakam with thin blade, straight
first, then with a sharp curve towards the end, with three jingles
attached. Carried by a NAYAR, during the procession in honour of
the goddess Bhagavati. Pitt-Rivers Museum, University of Oxford,
1920.55.16.

society with rites that may well lead back to the tradition of the Classical mysteries, examples of which are known from the Near East and Mediterranean. When more orthodox rites are required, they must delegate this to the Namboodiris. From this, one can surmise that truth is overlaid by lots of subsequent propaganda and reframing.

Pattini's story is the basis of the famous religious narrative called the *Tale of the Anklet* (Tamil: *Shilappu-adikaram*). Although not strictly speaking counted as "canonical" religious scripture, it is one of the five great epic works of Tamil culture and held in very high regard. Its author is said to be Illanko *Atikal* - whose name indicates he was one of the ancestors of the class of *Atikals* who are putative owners of the temple. This is yet another connection between the story of Pattini and the temple at Kotunkolur. Atikal must once have been a common name for a Buddhist or Jaina notable.

In the western yard of the temple at Kotunkolur is a small, almost insignificant hut built of laterite. It houses a deity called *Vasuurimaala* whose name means "garland of smallpox", perhaps a shocking name for a goddess! This kind of deity is not uncommon in many countries and is sometimes referred to by anthropologists as a disease entity, somewhat akin to a *demon*. There is something about disease that invariably means such entities are believed to have magical powers. These days the priestesses of this cult are local *Naayar* women. This is an old clan, whose members worship serpents. Their social structure is also unusual by Indian standards as inheritance of names and family wealth etc passes through the female line. That is to say the Naayar are matrilineal, an unusual arrangement that often goes together with polygamous marriage.

These Naayar women prepare a red potion of lime and turmeric called *kuruti,* a symbolic form of blood. When people make offerings at the shrine they do so in order to avoid the smallpox. In most other regions of India, it is the goddess Kali who performs this role. Her substitution here can be explained by an episode in the *Tale of the Anklet* when Pattini subdues a demon called *Vasuurimaala.* This entity is not found anywhere else in India and therefore it can only be another survival from the Isis/Pattini cult.

This theme of curing disease is reiterated in many other festival songs collected locally. In this connection, I draw the readers attention to the Velan, a caste of local devil dancers, sorcerers and what orientalist Thurston[1] called "quack" doctors. One of their songs tells of the marriage of Kollam, which scholars say is another name for Pattini, and husband Conat. The goddess to be did not care for the

---

1.　E Thurston *Castes and Tribes of Southern India,* Madras, 1909

groom arranged for her by her family. Such was Kollam's mood that she cursed Conat thus: "may you be hanged without being killed for a theft you didn't commit", which is pretty much the fate that did befall Pattini's husband.[1]

The idea of conjugal bed as a place of magical danger is actually fairly universal idea in India and indeed in the Near East. Ancient Vedic texts, which perhaps span both domains, tell of how the blood of defloration can rise up and become an entity dangerous to the husband: "It becomes a magic spirit walking on feet, and like the wife it draws near the husband."[2]

Kollam/Pattini also rages against her uncle who made the match and tricks him, first decapitating then gouging out his eyes which become two stars, one called the "eight hour". This jolly song is sung over a multi-coloured chalk image of the goddess. She is thus also a disease entity associated with smallpox. The happy ending is achieved when she creates a manikin out of straw which she then resurrects.

Goddess Rites

The question that springs to mind is whether, there are any ritual activity at the temple that might be survivals from

---

1. Quoted in Obeyesekere (1984 : 543)
2. Atharva Veda 10.85.29 quoted in Doniger (2009 : 126)

those magical disease entities of the Near East, or even from the cult of Isis. It has been suggested that they might give new insight into some of the more secret practices of the Near Eastern mystery cults. It so happens that two very unusual festivals are celebrated at Kotunkolur. The first of these is the famous *Atukul Pongala* which occurs on a Full Moon in the month of March. This is a rite of cooking magick repleat with an obvious re-enactment of elements of the Pattini myth cycle. In annual festivities at Kotunkolur, the kindling of individual fires and the making of a porridge whose main ingredients are water, rice and jaggery, still constitutes a central component of the popular cult rites. So popular is this ritual it even creates a tangible effect on the local air supply. Here is an account of the cooking ritual called a Pongala (rice pudding) performed as an offering to Bhadrakali at the Kotunkolur temple. Its author incidentally found that women of the cult and indeed women in Kerala in general enjoyed greater sexual equality and freedom than elsewhere in India.

The ritual is timed to a recitation of the epic drama; a moment in the rite when Pattini tears off her breast and sets fire to the city of Madurai. At this moment the priests in the temple kindle the first fire and it is passed hand to hand until many thousands of readily prepared cooking fires have been kindled:

"I stand in the sun, waiting with the hundreds of

thousands of other women for the moment to light my fire. The air is filled with the sounds of the women ululating, bells are ringing, the sound of firecrackers and drums is deafening, as the fire comes down the line from the temple, passed from woman to women. I reach over the coconut fronds I am holding and put them into the flames of the fire held by the woman next to me. After bending over and igniting my own cooking fire. I turn to Elinor so she can light her fire from mine. Immediately the air is filled with the smoke and heat of hundreds of thousands of coconut fires. Smoke, how do I describe the smoke? I have never experienced anything like it. It is burning hot, white, thick smoke, I try to breathe through the upper cloth of my mundu. This seems to help some and I see that other women are also breathing through their clothes. I try to cover my eyes because I am blinded by tears, but I have to watch the Pongala pot, and I am afraid that if I cannot see I will get my mundu too close and set myself on fire. Somehow I am breathing, and stirring and surviving this. Women tell me that they feel exhilarated later and that out temperatures go up so high it kills the small pox and chicken pox. The wind shifts and I can breathe again." [1]

The traditional rice of Kerala is red, or at least reddish, as if splattered with a red substance. See Judy Grahn's *metaformic* theory and ideas about *cosmetikos,* which is about the way biological colours resurface in our religious rites. When the ingredients boil over one knows the goddess has accepted the offering. In a final act, the priests *asperge* the pots with

1.   Dianne Jenett "Red Rice for Bhagavati" *ReVision*, Winter 1998 v20 i3 p37

rose water and contents are taken home to share with family members. As they return, the women celebrants are showered with flower petals which is in itself very reminiscent of the classical story where the eating of flowers transforms Lucius back into human form. This rite is the antithesis of the rites of the following lunar month when pongala is prohibited. What follows is the very controversial, for some, Bharani ritual in the same temple.

Disgracing the Goddess

The details of this ritual are controversial and often provoke letters of complaint to the local press and even street protests. *The Hindu* newspaper of 24th March 2004 reported 'The rites also protest against some of the established religious practices. "The worship is 'tamasic', a celebration of raw and untamed energy, an expression of repressed power," said E. K. Ravi, secretary, Kshetra Kshema Samithy.'

On the face of it the festival re-enacts the conflict between the goddess Kali and a demon called Darukan. The beginning of the rite is signalled by the Bharani star, the second of 27 lunar mansions. The mansions or houses are formed by the division of the path of the Moon around the Earth, hence each mansion correspondes to one lunar day. This whole system is very similar to the ancient Egyptian conception of lucky and unlucky days. In 2015 the rite occurred on 23

March, just after the New Moon of Aquarius.

Indian astrology, like its classical Greek antecedent, is sidereal. That is to say, it calculates the signs of the zodiac based upon the actual position of the stars. Over the last 2000 years the signs have actually 'slipped back' due to a phenomenon known as precession of the equinoxes. In the West, following the fall of paganism, there occurred a *caesura* between our intellectual life and the sources of astrology lore; consequently the signs remained fixed as they were 2000 years ago. So for example, to make an approximate conversion of your current Sun sign to its equivalent in the sidereal system, one must add 6 degrees to it's position as given in the ephemeris and then subtract one whole zodiacal sign. So for example for someone born early march, their Sun sign will be given as 10 degrees Pisces. But the table will be using the nominal or *tropical* data. Convert to sidereal will be 16 degrees Aquarius!

The Bharani rite marks the beginning of the hot summer before the coming of the monsoon rains. The Bharani star is represented by a hearth or a fireplace and also by an earthenware pot, that some say is homologous to the female sexual organ or yoni.[1] The symbol of Aquarius is also a pot and this perhaps emphasizes the same symbolism. The rituals occur over the entire lunar month, beginning at dawn with a symbolic pollution of the temple, which is circled three times by a member of the caste of goldsmiths ringing a bell, a clear reference to the goldsmith who in the old story, falsely accuses Pattini's husband of theft. After this action, life in the temple continues apparently as before for a little while. The floors are swept and the Brahmins continue with their daily liturgy. But then the world of the temple is turned upside down for the remainder of the lunar month.

For the final week of the lunar month none of the normal rites can be performed due to the existing and imminent pollution of the shrine. The suspension of normal services includes rites such as the *Pongala* described earlier, but also Kathakali dance dramas and the ritual use of *kuruti* (a deep red potion made from turmeric and lime juice). All this stops.

Instead several non-orthodox rites occur. The mysterious society of Atikals, whose condition we discussed earlier, now return to the temple and conduct their own secret rites mostly behind closed doors. The only known detail of these rites is inferred from the condition of the cult image of Bhadra-Kali, which has been freshly smeared with sandalwood paste.

The most important day in this time of 'misrule' occurs in

---

1.   M J Gentes "Scandalizing the Goddess at Kodungallur" *Asian Folklore Studies*, volume 51 (1992 : 301)

the last week of the lunar month, with activities reaching a crescendo during its final twelve hours. Hundred of thousands of devotees appear from all over Kerala. Press reports speak of a crush that in one year reached 500,000 visitors. Some of these special religious societies circumambulate the temple. The prelude to these special days, is the signal opening of a red umbrella, and the raising of the red banner on the temple flagpole. The devotees circumambulate the temple, eventually racing in a gnostic frenzy, often bleeding from self-inflicted wounds. They sing scandalous songs with lines such as those quoted earlier. No one is spared ridicule of an overtly sexual nature. A great deal of alcohol and no doubt other drugs are consumed.

Some of the devotees carry two sticks which they use in their dancing, others brandish the sickle sword. Most of these pilgrims are non Brahmin ritual specialists such as the already mentioned Atikals but also the *Veliccappadu*. These Veliccappadu, whose name means "a channel who sheds light" are spirit mediums, men and women, followers of Kali who utter oracles when in trance. They dress in red, wear heavy anklets and bells and wield the sickle sword. The sword is used by them to scoop a pile of mixed grains from a bucket and transfer them into the hands of a devotee, who then tosses them toward the divine image.

In the Northwest of the temple is a tower with a gaping

mouth; a tongue-like red banner hangs from its lattice. Devotees who cannot go inside, fling their offerings into its mouth, turmeric packets, coconuts, coins and even live chickens! The Nayar people sacrifice cockerels, hence the alternative name of this festival is Cock Festival. There are special offering stones near the walls of the inner courtyard for this purpose. You might well empathise with these creatures whose blood soon covers the inner courtyard of the temple.

The female veliccappadu have special initiations into the mysteries of the goddess. Because of this, they are able to produce oracles for clients, predicting the future but also providing reassurance, chastisement, and one presumes even help resolve disputes. This manifestation of oracles at a mass festival is a pattern very much evident in Egyptian temple practice. In fact, consultation of an oracle is pretty much the defining feature of Egyptian temple practice. This is reenacted in the story quoted earlier, when the character Lucius confronts the priests carrying the image of the goddess Isis and is then miraculously cured of his affliction.

Whilst all this is going on outside the temple, a snaking line of pilgrims has made its way inside for "darshan"; the characteristic activity of Hindu temple life involving a brief meeting with the goddess, the making of an offering and in

The velichappadu photographed by
Challiyil Eswaramangalath Pavithran Vipin (Creative commons)

The velichappadu photographed by
Challiyil Eswaramangalath Pavithran Vipin (Creative commons)

return the receipt of a blessing (prasad). As these devotees move through the packed spaces they chant:

"Amme! Amme! Amme! Amme!"

"Mother! Mother! Mother! Mother!"[1]

After all this activity the temple is swept clean and then closed to the public for a further seven days, the priesthood continuing with their regular cult practice undisturbed. The resident goddess of the temple is allowed to rest, which she is in dire need having been strongly agitated by the festival activities not to mention the takeover of the space by numerous demons. These intrusions subject the temple to such an onslaught the goddess is said to be in an overstimulated, satiated condition due to the enormous quantities of blood offerings.

There are several theories as to why this strange interaction occurs, but a good one advanced by Induchudan, is that the underlying focus of the Bharani festival is the original cult of Pattini, whom we have identified as a form of Isis. In a sense it is a temporary reclaiming of the shrine by the remnants of her original devotees. The focus of the rite, would have been the secret chamber, which the candidate entered and then re-emerged through the tunnel reborn.

---

1.   Gentes (1992).

The opening of the umbrella, the pollution and the frenzied run, all centre on the eastern, largely unused portico which is really the home of Pattini. The Left breast is also said in Tantrik lore to be the seat of a woman's *shakti* power. Thus, women pilgrims do expose their breasts whilst singing and chanting in the festival.

Almost all scholarly commentators agree that there is something extremely heterodox, perhaps even alien in the ritual activities at this temple. Many, such as Obeyesekere in passages discussed earlier, ascribe all this to the influence of the Syrian cult of Attis and the goddess Cybele. My own research tends to confirm the views of Richard Fynes[1] in placing Isis as a much better fit. That this is routinely overlooked is nothing new, Egyptology has suffered from limited, even puritanical interpretations of its ritual activity. Modern research is revealing a much more *raunchy* temple culture.

Let me start this comparison of the two temple traditions with something I have drawn attention to before. Those accounts of ancient travellers, beginning with a famous description from Herodotus, that presents quite a bawdy picture of the vibe at Egyptian festivals, such as this from the temple of Bast, one of several feline goddesses.

---

1.   Richard Fynes (1993 : 386)

"When the people are on their way to Bubastis they go by river, men and women together, a great number of each in every boat. Some of the women make a noise with rattles, others play flutes all the way, while the rest of the women, and the men, sing and clap their hands. As they journey by river to Bubastis, whenever they come near any other town they bring their boat near the bank; then some of the women do as I have said, while some shout mockery of the women of the town; others dance, and others stand up and expose themselves. ... But when they have reached Bubastis, they make a festival with great sacrifices, and more wine is drunk at this feast than in the whole year beside. Men and women (but not children) are wont to assemble there to the number of seven hundred thousand, as the people of the place say."
Bk II 60-61

This is riotous behaviour en route to a festival. It seems likely that the party did not end at the temple gates; records show there were at least three annual feasts of drunkenness celebrating the seasonal 'return' of the goddess Hathor/ Sekhmet to Egypt. One of the epithets of this goddess is "She before whom everyone performs sexual intercourse".[1] These feasts are recorded on temple calendars for 1st Thoth (July), 20th Thoth (July) and 5 Paopi (August). Scholars

---

1. Mark Smith & Richard Jasnow "As for Those Who have called me Evil, Mut will Call them Evil: Orgiastic Cultic Behaviour and its Critics in Ancient Egypt" *Enchoria* 32 (2010/2011 : 49)

such as Professor Mark Smith see no reason to think this wasn't a regular feature of religious life.

Bast has a particularly bawdy reputation but there is also in Herodotus his recollection of a festival, this time in honour of the Hippopotamus, which he says was the sacred animal of Papremis, a lost location somewhere in Egypt's delta region. The female Hippo is one of the important goddesses of Egypt. The scholar Gwyn-Griffiths argues that Ares, her son, is the Greek name of the god Horus. Isis is the mother of Horus, and therefore Hippo must be yet another of her avatars. Experts speculate on the meaning of the description, it could be a violent commemoration of the conflict between Horus and Seth or even Seth and a female Apophis, which also involves the theme of mother incest:

> "At Papremis sacrifice is offered and rites performed as elsewhere; but when the sun is sinking, while a few of the priests are left to busy themselves with the image, the greater number of them beset the entrance of the temple, with clubs of wood in their hands; [where] they are confronted by more than a thousand men, all performing vows, and carrying wooden clubs like the rest. The image of the god, in a little wooden gilt casket, is carried on the day before this from the temple to another sacred chamber.

The few who are left with the image draw a four-wheeled cart carrying it in its casket; the other priests stand in the temple porch and prevent its entrance; the votaries take the part of the god, and smite the priests, who resist. There is hard fighting with clubs and heads are broken, and as I think (though the Egyptian told me no life was lost), many die of their wounds. The assemblage, say the people of the country, took its rise thus: the mother of Ares dwelt in the temple; Ares had been reared away from her, and when he grew to manhood came to have intercourse with his mother; but as her attendants, never having seen him before, kept him off and would not suffer him to pass. Ares brought men from another town, roughly handled the attendants and gained access to his mother. From this, they say, arose this custom of a battle of blows at the festival in honour of Ares."

Herodotus II: 63

There are other examples from Egypt that seem similar in vibe to the "disgracing the goddess" festival found in India. Thus the festival calendar of Esna, house of ancient goddess Neith, together with her consort Khnum & their child Heka, has space for something called the "seizing the staffs" which could well be like that Papremis rite described above.

Recent research has tended to reveal a far less puritanical image of Egyptian temple practice. The title of a recent article by Professors Mark Smith & Richard Jasnow was sufficiently startling to make waves on the Internet.

"As for Those Who have called me Evil, Mut will Call them Evil: Orgiastic Cultic Behaviour and its Critics in Ancient Egypt" *Enchoria* 32 2010/2011pp9-53. See http://www.livescience.com/23401-cult-fiction-ancient-egypt-priest.html September 24, 2012 reported as " 'Cult Fiction' Traced to Ancient Egypt Priest".

Mixing sex and religion was obviously an issue in the ancient world, and Egyptians in the Roman period were keen to finesse rumours of such activity. This they did in reaction to the perceived puritanism of their new masters. Hence discussion of the practice was hidden in the form of a story, as in "I once heard" etc. This suppression of "tantrik" aspects of ancient religion is something also familiar in the western study of Indian religion which posed something of a dilemma for western scholars confronted with overt sexual imagery. The same inhibitions were manifest during the early days of Egyptology, whose exponents tended to suppress and ignore things that made them uncomfortable.

The authors of the article contend that it was the sexual component of Egyptian rites rather than the drunkenness that was problematic. There is a very famous annual "feast of drunkenness" celebrated all over Egypt on the 20th day of a month known as Thoth. Just like the "Disgracing the Goddess" festival in India, this one celebrates the return of the goddess after an absence. This return is no doubt connected to the *return* of the Sothis star, a personification of the goddess Isis, which is invisible in the night sky for a long period; its return coinciding with the beginning of the Egyptian new year.

Professors Smith & Jasnow translated this revealing ancient text:

"I will sing, I will become drunk, I being before Mut [the mother goddess] daily, the priests will come, the singers who renders joyful the countenance of everyone who comes in order to worship [the Ka] of the divine image of the *merer* goddess ... the mistress. Drink truly, Eat truly, Sing truly. Don clothing, anoint yourself, adorn the eyes and enjoy sexual bliss. Those who have proclaimed Mut to you, those who have proclaimed to you the goddess say 'she will not let you be distant from drunkenness on any day. She will not allow you to be lacking in any manner, you will spend a lifetime, all your limbs being healthy. You will be like me at all times. As for those who have called me evil. Mut will call them evil. ...' [1]

There is a line further in the same text which reads *t3 sšf3(t) mḥ-3.t.* "The third story" which marks this out as some sort of anecdote or perhaps extracts from a popular story. What we see here is likely a recollection by priests of a story or anecdote, which is framed in such a way so as to enable them to distance themselves from the narrative, rather in the way of "I have heard such and such a story" concerning activities in the temple. Rather like the account of the Hindu temple written by Induchudan it enables them to record something that may be taboo but is rightly debated

---

1.   Smith & Jasnow (2010/2011 : 32)

or critiqued. The tone is not prescriptive and is likely written about Egyptians by other Egyptians.

Several versions of this were found, all most likely a specific temple hymn adapted by other cults. All concern the "rites of a goddess whose devotees worship her with musick, feasting, drunkenness and acts of sexual intercourse, by which they hope to see her in a vision. This divinity is the eye of the sun god, his daughter, the uraeus who protects him, the visible manifestation of his dazzling brilliance and embodiment of the fiery blast of his heat. She personifies a cosmic force of unlimited power, and is therefore very dangerous. But her power is not invariably destructive, it can be harnessed for beneficial purposes, manifesting itself for instance in the form of erotic energy. Consequently, the goddess has an ambivalent character, ferocious at some times but mild and gentle at others. Her rites are intended to pacify or appease her, ensuring that her gentle side is to the fore." [1]

The venue for this was a special room near the entrance to the temple. The timing either connected with the return of the star Sothis or perhaps some point in the solar cycle, either the solstice or equinox. An inscription on the Ptolemaic gate of the temple of Mut at Karnak refers to such a hall in

---

1.   Smith & Jasnow (2010/2011 : 37)

which dances were performed as part of the goddess' cult. This is a continuation of a long tradition of similar architectural spaces; such as a New Kingdom "columned porch of drunkenness."[1] These multi columned courtyards and halls are said to symbolize marshland. The marshland has many complex layers of meaning to the Egyptian for instance "roaming the marshes" was a common euphemism for sexual pleasure. Hence a coffin lid of Ptolemaic scribe Wennofer has a long panagyric which includes the lines: "I was a lover of drink, a lord of the feast day, it was my passion to roam the marshes."[2]

---

1.   Smith & Jasnow (2010/2011 : 42)

2.   M Lichthelm, *Ancient Egyptian Literature III The Late period*, (0000 : 54sq)

The Tale of the Anklet

"...I would argue that the remarkable similarities between the witchcraft lore of Somadeva's 'Barber's Tale' *and allied Asian traditions on the one hand, and that of the Roman *striges* and allied European traditions on the other, cannot be adequately explained on the basis of coincidental, independent innovation by cultures across the globe." [1]

"The Tale of the Anklet", (Sanskrit *Shilappattikaram)* is one of five celebrated epic poems of Tamil Nadu. It was written between the years 500-900 of our era. It could be viewed as the Indian version of the story of Isis & Osiris. To set the scene, here is a description of the two central characters, Pattini and Palanga. Here we see them in their home town, a place they knew before their lives were transformed by the dramatic events of the story.

"The sun shone over the open terraces, over the alehouses, near the harbours and over the turrets with their air holes looking like the eyes of deer. In different

---

1. David Gordon White "Yogini Dakini Pairika, Strix: Adventures in Comparative Demonology" (SERAS) Southeast Review of Asian Studies, Vol 35 (2013 : 16). [In the tale, the barber convinces the king that his wife, with whom the king has been enjoying an illicit affair, is in fact a witch (dakini) who will slowly suck the life out of him as she has already done to the barber.]

places of Puhar the onlookers attention was arrested by
the sight of *Yavanas* (Greeks, Foreigners, Arabs, Syrians,
Jews, Westerners) whose prosperity was never on the
wane. On the harbours were to be seen sailors, come
from distant lands, but for all the appearances they lived
as one community ... in certain places weavers were seen
dealing in fine fabrics made of silk, fur and cotton.
Whole streets were full of silks, corals, sandal and myrrh,
besides a wealth of rare ornaments, perfect pearls, gems
and gold, which were beyond reckoning ." [1]

All versions of the story say Pattini and her husband were
from the wealthy merchant class who owned ships. This
was a time when Buddhist or Jaina faiths dominated in the
region. Merchants could happily belong to either religion, as
indeed could foreign converts. Such people might have
complex religious identities, continuing their allegiance to
a mystery cult from the land of their birth whilst
supplementing this with an allegiance to the religion of their
adopted country. This kind of behaviour was and is common
enough. Even today, people of the region convert to
Buddhism whilst retaining native animistic beliefs.[2] Some
Jaina devotees of the time, combined their faith with the
practice of astrology, occultism and what some call

---

1.   V. R. Ramachandra, Dikshitar *The Silappadikaram*,
      (1939 : 110-111)
2.   Obeyesekere (1984 : 533)

demonology; all things which were part of the international culture of the time.[1]

In this world, the worship of a Near Eastern mother goddess would not be taboo within India or the mindset of the time. Such beliefs might actually have found fertile ground in India and could easily be assimilated with native cults such as that of the goddess Pattini. There would be no need for those who espoused Near Eastern beliefs to keep them secret nor need they exist in a ghetto or as an enclave of the "great tradition". At that time they were free to merge with native religion.

Once upon a time, so the Indian story tells us, a goddess took human birth in the form of the maiden Pattini. When the time came for her marriage, her parents arranged a suitable match with a local family; who in return offered their handsome son Palanga. However Palanga was a bit of a playboy and was not faithful to his goddess wife. A love triangle developed between the virginal Pattini, the fickle

1.   see R N Nandi 1973, *Religious institutions and cults in the Deccan, c. A.D. 600-A.D. 1000*

husband and the beautiful temptress, perhaps 'whore', who in our story is called Madhavi.[1]

In some contexts Madhavi is also considered to be a divine entity; her name occurs in Tantrik texts where she is viewed as a 'Yogini' or witch: "There is no Yoni on Earth resembling the beautifully rounded Yoni of Madhavi," says the *YoniTantra*, "nor the firmness of her breasts."[2] In the Mahabharata she is described as the polyandrous woman who sells herself several times over to a succession of Kings in exchange for many hundreds of horses; miraculously restoring her virginity after each encounter.

In our story the beautiful Madhavi is said to be a courtesan, skilled in all of the sixty-four arts of lovemaking and, also interestingly, of rhetoric. The price of possessing this lovely creature was set as her entire weight in gold! Palanga, hopelessly smitten, agreed, although this was virtually his wife & his entire fortune.

Palanga and the courtesan Madhavi eventually quarrel and Palanga abandons her and returns, penniless, to his faithful

1.   Obeyesekere 1984 : 479

2.   *YoniTantra* IV Patala translated by Shri Lokanath

wife Pattini. They are now in dire need of funds. The all suffering Pattini agrees to sell one of her precious jewels, the golden anklet of the story. The couple leave their home town and travel to distant Madurai, famous for its gold merchants, where they hope to sell discretely, the valuable ornament.

In the Egyptian 'original', Osiris, the husband of Isis, also has an extra-marital affair with Underworld goddess Nephthys, the wife of the god Seth. In both narratives, sexual jealousy is one of the engines of the story; among the Egypt devotees of Seth, this is viewed as the motive for Seth's murderous rage against Osiris. Palanga will eventually suffer a similar fate to Osiris, dismembered, decapitated and depending on the reading of certain other features of the story, castrated.

The 'Virgin' Goddess

The idea that Isis was a 'virgin' goddess is based on a famous passage in Plutarch's book *Isis & Osiris*, "At Sais the seated statue of Athena, whom they consider to be Isis also, bore the following inscription: 'I am all that has been and is and will be; and no mortal has ever lifted my mantle.'[1] In fact

---

1. Plutarch *Isis & Osiris*, translated by Gwyn-Griffiths edition 354b-c chapter 9 (pp131)

Plutarch has got the story wrong, the major goddess of Sais in the Egyptian delta was actually Neith. Neith is an ancient warrior goddess said to be of uncertain gender, i.e., having 'male' strengths. Her threat is no idle boast. Gwyn-Griffiths agrees that the reference to lifting her mantle is clearly sexual, and it is echoed in a magical papyrus of the time of Hadrian:

"[Isis] Holy maiden, give me a sign things are going to happen, reveal your holy veil, shake your black [Tyche =fortune] and move the constellation of the bear." [1]

So this idea certainly is part of the later Egyptian tradition although on the face of it, it is contradictory to the role of Isis as mother of Horus; as indeed is the idea of Pattini as wife of Palanga. But maybe we can resolve this paradox when we consider that the conception of Horus is itself unusual. Horus is conceived after the death of his putative father Osiris. Moreover Osiris has been emasculated by Seth. The magic prowess of Isis in part is derived from her response to her husband's injuries. She uses magic to resuscitate Osiris, including his damaged generative organs. Isis could therefore still be considered a virgin goddess

---

1.   PGM 57, 16-17

despite the post-mortem conception.[1] Egyptian Isis & Hindu Pattini share much the same vibe, some versions of the Indian myth say her marriage to Palanga was regular, others say that any lack of consummation of the marriage was due to his impotence.

In Apuleius' *Isis Book*, chastity is mentioned as a quality of the goddess that initiates were also required to in some way emulate. The following speech is addressed by Isis to the character Lucius, and adjures him to be in a chaste state. Other sources of the time show that the requirement would only have been for a limited period. This temporary chastity in the classical world is more like the attitude that prevailed in Indian yoga. Chastity is a specific practice and not necessarily a permanent sacerdotal state:

"...with different service, religious tendance and constant chastity, know that I alone have power to prolong your life also beyond the span determined by your destiny."[2]

Gwyn-Griffiths, the translator of *The Isis Book*, explains that this is a temporary period of chastity, usually of ten days duration. Other passages from the Classics back this up.

---

1. Gwyn-Griffiths *De Iside et Osiride* (1970 : 284)
2. Gwyn-Griffiths, (1975) *The Isis Book (Apuleius of Madauros, Metamorphoses*, Bk XI, Chapter 6, section 271, line 5.

The complete rule of the cult is set out in *The Isis Book* chapter 23. Similar rules applied to initiates of the Attis cult, who observed sexual abstinence during the nine days of the spring mysteries; enough to prompt numerous complaints from frustrated husbands.[1] There is little or no evidence in ancient Egyptian records for perpetual chastity. The vast majority of the Egyptian priesthood was drawn from the general populace on a rotational basis. Chastity and abstinence were required only during one's period of service and perhaps only then in certain areas of the temple.

Of course the goddess herself may well endure a more stringent self-imposed regime. In Classical iconography Isis is the paradigmatic *mater dolorosa*, bewailing her husband and defending her child Horus. Isis gives birth just the once, but the unnatural manner of the conception of Horus makes him a vulnerable, weakling child. Although Isis may technically be virginal, this does not mean her myth is asexual. Far from it, there is a great deal of sex in her entire myth cycle.

Indian Pattini never conceives and this points to another shared theme this time concerning male spouses, who for various reasons are challenged in this area; Osiris because of the loss of his penis (and arguably testicles). Pattini's

1.   Gwyn Griffiths (1975 : 355fn)

husband Palanga never consummates their marriage. This is a precursor of his castration during his fated execution.

Perhaps it is time to look at the source of one of her myths. I've already mentioned many times the epic *Shilappattikaram : the tale of the Anklet*. This long work inspired many shorter songs and ritual dramas. It is one of these relatively short ritual dramas that I want now to examine in detail. The following is the complete text of a twentieth century performance recorded by eminent anthropologist Gunanath Obeyesekere. He has very kindly granted me permission to reproduce this complete transcription from his monumental study *The Goddess Pattini*.[1] Obeyesekere confirms that this is probably one of the last such performances, as modernism has overtaken the culture and rendered the tradition moribund. Even so, it demonstrates a remarkable survival of an ancient tradition:

This is ritual drama, designated "maraa ipaddiima" or "killing and resurrection", was recorded in the Hindu community of Sri Lanka. It requires an audience and a performance area. Some of the action is narrated, some is acted out. Music, song and dance are vital elements of the ritual.

---

1.   Gunanath Obeyesekere, *The Cult of the Goddess Pattini* (Chicago 1984 : 245-273)

The Myths of the Pattini Cycle

1.   Gracious Pattini known throughout the world
      Gives the young Palanga, her good husband
      Her priceless anklet to be sold.[1]
      She thrusts the anklet in his hand.

2.   He puts the anklet in his pouch and ties it
      Its price is truly inestimable.
      Studded with gems and stones of two thousand colors
      At its base this gem anklet has of gold, many pounds.[1]

3.   As if sensing the death that waits him
      The attractive Palanga took the anklet
      -A goldsmith had an enmity from a previous birth-[2]
      He thought: let me go to the city of Madura.

---

1. Obeyesekere says anklet weight is 40lbs! (8000 = kalans = 40 grains).

2. It might seem a *non sequitor* but in this one line the poem evokes a doctrine that any Indian audience would accept as self-evidently true. As validated in early Ayurvedic medical texts, if in this life, you encounter someone who harbours a seemingly irrational enmity against you, the explanation might be that you were enemies in a previous life.

4. Her beloved Palanga took the anklet
    Full of sorrow at the thought of leaving
    -all due to the past enmity of a goldsmith-
    He prepared to leave for the city of Madura.

5. "Your virtues spread like the shimmering Moon
    O lord full of auspiciousness and charm
    What will become of me when you're gone
    Where shall I stay when you aren't here?"

6. Both of us have come together from our native land
    My tears," he said, "prevent me from sleeping
    Do not go here and there O gracious Pattini
    Stay here while I come back to you."

7. "Oh lady possessed of bounteous kindness and glory
    I shall not sleep, my eyes won't close
    Till I return after leaving you today
    O king YA, she is in your charge."

8. "You did not listen to my words
    With your own hands promise me
    To go see the undying, powerful king
    And come back to me in haste."

9. "We left the city of Kaveri where we lived
    Bereft of our kinsmen, and in a strange land

They were stricken with sorrow for their children
How hard it was to leave them and go."

10. "Blue lotuses[1] opening in the dawn
Auspicious flowers with blue lotus hues
Sal flowers, and golden petals in the dawn
May your journey be as pleasant."

11. Thus Pattini said worshipping his feet
Tears flowed from her eyes, a shower after a drought
"Kind and living lord be careful
As you go past paths and streets."

12. "If you see someone with goodness and generosity
Give him the anklet and ask for its value
But if you see those cunning goldsmiths
Don't join hands with them, those cobras."

13. "With firm resolve like a single tree I lived
Together unseparated from him till now

---

1. Blue Lily or *Nymphaea caerulea* is another interesting link
with Egypt. The plant is not a native Indian botanical, but
is an import from the Nile valley where it is emblematic
of Upper Egypt. It has well-known narcotic properties.
The use of this herb is attested in other tantrik texts. (See
Morgan, *Supernatural Assault in Ancient Egypt*, (Mandrake
2011)

Till he comes back from Madura's[1] kingdom
When will I see him again?"

14. "Like people making joyful love constantly
We enjoyed prosperity in one bed together[2]
When you go my breast will be empty
Lord without you how shall I live?"

15. "My beloved lord, loving and kind
Cannot you see the mountain fire of my pain?
See how I implore you with my cries
Alas, alas, to whom shall I tell my sorrow?"

16. Possessed of dainty feet and eyes and body
Pattini the decorous noble lady then
Gave, with proper thoughts, to Palanga
Cooked rice and vegetables to carry.

17. "O my good lord speaker of loving words

---

1. Madura or Madurai, still a major city in Tamil Nadu, its streets radiate out like lotus petals from the famous Meenakshi Amman Temple, the local name of Parvati, consort of Shiva.

2. Implying that their relationship was sexual although other versions of the myth do not.

I have come with you to this place
But now you go on to a distant land, my lord
How can my breast take this pain?"

18. "My eyes a dam holding back a stream of
falling water
My shoulders a shade held over my sorrowing breast
My hands a battle stick held aloft
But my mind a firm Meru rock that cannot be
cleaved."

19. "A herd that comes down to rest
is easily captured, my beloved
And owing to the nature of harlots
ne'er look at them, go your way."[1]

---

1. Pattini now recalls verses from an omen text, warning
Palanga to take note of certain signs which may indicate
problems ahead. The first omen refers to her love rival,
the harlot Madhavi, the cause of their current impoverish-
ment.

Omens

20.   "These sayings coming down from old times
       Truths handed down in our country
       If you care for me listen lord
       If you see omens do not make the trip."

21.   "Women with empty hands and empty pots
       Dumb one, deaf and blind, and lame
       It's inauspicious to see these on your journey.[1]
       Which then will become fruitless.

22.   "Red flowers and cruel 'torture flowers' if you see
       Or come across a snakeskin in your path
       If someone confronts you and asks you
       where you're bound
       These are omens listed from old times."

---

1.   These are old superstitions, not very politically correct. In
      the Indian popular view, disability could be seen as a result
      of a bad action in a past life. In Egyptian omen texts,
      dreaming one sees oneself with a disability was a bad
      omen, although such people were well treated in everyday
      life. Seeing oneself as a dwarf was a bad omen because it
      indicated one was somehow diminished. Archaeological
      records in Egypt show that dwarfs lived quite fulfilled
      lives.

23.   "Here's a truth coming from old times
        If gecko lizards and woodpeckers screech
        Or you see Vaddas (hunters) come from
        Ruhuna (the South) direction
        You see danger then, they are obstacles [omens]."

24.   "If you see, in your journey, signs of lizards
        Cobras fighting and pigeons and crows
        or deer cross from right to left
        Don't take the journey, if you love me lord."

25.   "The cries of a peacock, woodpecker and owl
        Cobras, rat snakes and *hers* of marsh deer
        Foxes, mongooses, and hare, if you see
        Don't go, dear lord, it bodes no good."

26.   "If the earth in anger trembles
        The skies thunder and down comes the rain
        If you see these happen
        There's no point in your journey."

27.   "Old men living like paupers
        Men with noses cut off, crippled hands and feet
        If you see soldiers or thieves with weapons
        Take not the trip lest you meet death."

28.   "But if you see these beautiful things

Like women nursing infants, saying loving words
It's a good sign to see them on your trip
Wherever you go, it'll be auspicious."

29.   "Respected lord possessed of much tenderness
       Remember well my loving words"
       Then Pattini's husband, full of good qualities
       Took his leave by pressing her breasts
       and kissing them.

30.   Like the ocean waves bursting on the shore
       Tears streamed from Pattini's eyes.
       A strange sorrow flamed in her body
       As she gave Palanga permission to depart.

31.   Exalted Pattini advised him thus
       And tied the anklet in his pouch
       Then the noble lord of the virtuous Pattini
       Got ready to depart.

32.   He did not heed the words
       of Pattini filled with reasonableness.
       Several days the merchant travelled
       In spite of seeing bad omens.

33.   The sun's rays hid under the tree's shade
       Flashing turtles sported in the waters

See the many-plumaged birds bathe -
These he saw in a beautiful lake.

34.   He rested himself and got ready to eat
He found lotus leaves to serve as plates
Then Palanga sat under a shade
And got ready to eat rice and curries.

35.   Taking up the packet of rice to eat
He sprinkled water and praised the Buddha
He offered a portion to the gods
The prince then sat down to eat

36.   A crow[1] sat in the sun on a branch
He looked all around and grabbed some of his food
That low sinful creature,
Cawed three times loudly crying

---

1.   The crow, (Sanskrit: *Sakuni*) is thought to be a bird of ill omen, it even gives its name to a class of beings able to possess a person. Crows are considered unclean because they steal ritual offerings. A character in the great Indian epic *The Mahabharata* is called Sakuni, he is a master of dice, a common method of consulting omens. In the story his cheating at dice sets in motion a chain of events that leads to a great slaughter. A crow also plays a role in India's other great epic, the *Ramayana*. Egypt also has bird omens. The earliest mythology of Isis depicts her as one of the ominous birds that gather at any funeral (qv *Haert*).

37. The crow now climbed on a branch
    with the rice held in its beak
    [Palanga knew what these signs meant]
    Soon the crow flew away.

38. Knowing the danger he was in
    owing to the effect of bad time
    He gave some of his own blood to demons
    And some rice, and went his way.[1]

39. Singing pleasant songs he wound his way
    The youth's strength was sapped
    The noble one was sorely tired
    When he reached Madurai city.

40. Palanga did not tarry for long
    With the anklet in hand, in his innocence
    [to expiate the bad karma he'd gathered]
    Unknowingly reached the goldsmith's street.

---

1. to expiate or avert the effects of the bad omen Palanga makes a food offering to the malign spirits, cooked rice mixed with his own blood and formed into cakes. This kind of offering is fairly common in India. It is one of those universal magical practices, attested from folklore in Egypt also where such offerings to the gods were known from prehistory.

41.   His karma from previous births
        Now led him to Death himself
        Palanga, handsome of feature, that day
        Wended his way to the goldsmith's street.

42.   The cruel and bloody goldsmith
        To prevent Palanga from leaving soon
        Asked him courteously to be seated
        And inquired the price of the anklet.

43.   He filled his ears with honeyed words
        Then sitting in dignity weighed the anklet
        "I'll offer a good price for this, he told him"
        And swiftly ran to the king's palace.

44.   Pretending to go to a shop nearby
        He went to the king's assembly
        he clashed his hands, fell down, and moved backwards
        And spoke to the king of the sun dynasty.

45.   He bowed his head and worshipped the king
        "I remember the beautiful queen said
        That her beautiful anklet was stolen one day
        This day I've seen the anklet thief."

46.   "If you don't surround him
And hold him prisoner
The thief will soon hear rumors
And hide himself somewhere."

47.   The king's crafty wrestlers came
Up to the handsome Palanga
They abused him and beat him
And took him to the palace.

48.   A full moon handsome body
And a gold complexion
A blow bent that body in two
Then red eyes and bound hands.

49.   "The anklet I repaired
Here's the thief who stole it."
"I haven't even dreamed of theft."
"I've brought the thief that took it."

50.   "This thief craved the anklet and stole it
Famished with terrible greed."
Then the goldsmith-sorcerer said:
"It is true, I never tell lies."

51.   That sinful goldsmith lied
And destroyed the noble king

"This is the thief." He said.
"Hated by gods and men."[1]

52.　The hardened wrestlers now
　　　Stood all around him
　　　They grabbed the anklet from him
　　　They dragged him and tied him up.

53.　The goldsmith showed his duplicity
　　　He informed the Pandi king
　　　He brought the wrestlers
　　　"Now bind this wretched man."

54.　A large and eager bunch
　　　That day led Palanga south
　　　Tied up and drawn like an ox
　　　And presented to the king.

1.　The story alludes to a previous incident when the gold-
　　smith had repaired the queen's anklet, one can presume a
　　common element of a woman's attire. He claimed
　　someone had broken into his studio and stolen it. It
　　seems an unlikely coincidence that the thief would return
　　to try to sell it back. The infeasible nature of this story
　　serves to underline the lack of wisdom of the king when
　　he acts on such a trumped up accusation. The craft also
　　associated with Egyptian Seth, the murderer of Osiris.
　　Gold-smithing also takes us into the realm of alchemy, an
　　Egyptian art connected with sorcery.

55.   When Palanga was there in this wise
      And he saw the king of Pandi
      He bowed his head but worshipped not
      "Look at this thief's audacity."

56.   "Thief, why don't you worship
      This honored king of immeasurable goodness
      Mind pleasing in his worthiness
      The Pandi king of illimitable pre-eminence?"

57.   "Only to the Buddha and the Sangha
      My teachers and parents dear
      Even though you call me thief
      I'll not worship anyone else."

58.   The bonds were firm and tight
      So death may come for certain
      "Look he brags without paying obeisance
      Which in itself proves his guilt."

59.   "This anklet belongs to Pattini
      And not to the Pandi queen
      Listen Pandi to my words
      Else this assembly will be cursed."

60.   "Let the queen be summoned
      To examine the anklet

Tie up the thief again
Now let's ask the queen."

61. As the king said
     The queen was swiftly summoned
     Curtains were held around her
     And she seated there within.

62. The queen came to the royal house
     "Tell us gladly what you know."
     She was given the gold anklet
     And the thief was shown to her.

63. The queen, stately as a divine maiden
     Took the jeweled anklet in her hand
     As she held the fiery anklet
     Her hands were sorely burned.

64. "This anklet is not mine
     "It belongs to a Pattini with *tejas*[1]
     It's one she wears on her foot
     Dear lord doubt it not."

---

1. Here is the reference to a Pattini, a class of female
    supernaturals, perhaps like a Yogini. Tejas is a fiery
    magical power that magicians accumulate by their ascetic
    practices.

65. "Oh Pandi king, known the world over
     This is not my anklet, alas!
     If you execute this thief
     Our country will be utterly ruined."[1]

66. "Note these words I've spoken
     Pay them heed, doubt not
     If you now kill the thief
     Dire calamity will befall us."

67. "My queen what do you mean?
     Didn't we give you your anklet
     We've caught the thief with his goods
     Queen, is not this your anklet?"

68. "Why did you bring me here?
     Is it to display your might
     Do not display the thief
     It's wrong O Pandi king."

---

1. If the king fails to uphold dharma or justice it will have
    cosmic consequences and lead to ruin. This doctrine has a
    parallel in the Egyptian kings obligation to uphold the
    principle of Justice personified as the goddess Maat.

The Goldsmith
(trying to discredit the Queen)

69. "When they see the beauty of men
     Women will always lie
     How then can we believe you?
     Women are fickle things."[1]

70. The queen was fair and proper
     Her words will last long
     "Listen lord to my words
     That goldsmith did grave wrong."

71. "Words unkind and untruthful
     Were spoken by the goldsmith
     They'll cause great confusion, lord
     Desist, or you'll regret it later."

72. At the exalted queen's words
     The goldsmith was enraged
     He spoke to the Pandi king
     Urging him thus.

---

1. This goldsmith reveals his misogyny and bad character,
    accusing the queen of lying because she is physically
    attracted to Palanga. He also recounts various old wis-
    dom tales about the failings of women, all designed to
    undermine her character.

73.　　"Passionately in love with a thief
　　　　She laid for him a large sheet
　　　　This she did though of noble birth
　　　　She was a queen, yet she did wrong."

74.　　"Giving the sword to the thief
　　　　And the scabbard to her lord
　　　　Haven't you heard this old tale
　　　　Of women's wrongs."

75.　　"Lusting after a dwarf, a woman
　　　　Pushed the great bodhisattva from a rock
　　　　And greedily collected his head
　　　　She was a queen, yet she did wrong."

76.　　"Oh renowned Pandi king
　　　　Of pure and noble dynasty
　　　　Faultless women did you say?
　　　　Haven't you heard them gripe?"

77.　　"Infatuated by his beauty
　　　　She now says he's no thief
　　　　She knows you'd commit sin
　　　　She'd a queen yet she does wrong."

The King is persuaded

78. He listened to the goldsmith's words
    And was struck with rage
    He brought his elephant out[1]
    In order to kill the thief.

79. It was given toddy and liquors
    Sharpened tusks and foaming mouth!
    See how the goldsmith leads him in
    Without other's seeing him.

80. Like a wasp drawn to a scent
    He followed it wielding a big goad
    He beat it, till it dropped dung all over
    Uttering thunderous roars.

---

1. Elephants still play a role in the festivities at Kotunkolur,
   and interestingly there is one part of the compound on
   which they do not walk, supposedly because of danger to
   the underground tunnel, but also equally because of a
   taboo about walking near the place where Palanga died.

Triple Death[1]

81.   There was Palanga tied up
        And the elephant some distance away
        Then it was set loose
        to kill the faultless thief.

82.   It stood in front of Palanga
        And saw him lying there
        It let loose blood and dung
        Then fell down on the ground.

83.   Now the ignorant man in anger
        Went before the king
        He tapped the king's pride
        "Now send the lowly dogs."

84.   When they saw him, that pack
        They sniffed, and ran around him
        Then came near and kissed his feet
        And ran away, that lowly pack.

---

1.   Three attempts are made to kill Palanga. An ancient form mirrored in the triple death of Osiris who is drowned, burned and decapitated. Pattini is also said to be thrice born, the origin of another local myth cycle "shooting the mango" verse 17 (Obeyesekere 1984 : 229)

85.   "Why goldsmith won't you speak up
How shall we execute this thief?
In order to kill this thief
Whom shall we summon?"

86   "Tell me where a *maruva* lives"
"He lives somewhere near
A distance of fifteen miles."[1]
"Command him to come here."

87.   With hatred coming from past lives
The goldsmith uttered falsehoods
He stood before the king
"tomorrow I'll bring *maruva*."

88.   On the day he sent for *maruva*
The *maruva* was away from home
Though it was the height of noon
His wife was lying in bed.

89   While sleeping in her bed
She dreamed a dreadful dream

---

1.   A *maruva* is an executioner, but also one of the emissaries of death. He has much in common with the character of the Egyptian god Seth.

Her husband came home that day
And she told him her dream.

90.   The maruva's wife, a good woman
[even though she sleeps at noon]
Related to her husband
The dreadful dream she saw.

91.   "Lips like flower petals
Wife with golden body
As you lay in bed
What dreadful dream did you see?"

92.   "It thundered and poured forth fire
The golden dome collapsed
The palace destroyed by fire
These three things I dreamed."

93.   "Thunderbolts a fire that'll spread
The golden dome is a great king
Lightning is a queen
Danger awaits the city of Madurai."[1]

---

1.   Once again dreams play a key role in the unfolding of the story. Also the dreams of the executioner's wife parallel the role of Nephthys, sister of Isis and wife of Seth, who sides with Osiris against her husband Seth.

94.   Danger lies ahead, he thought.
      It's because of this dream
      That the great king of Pandi
      Sent messengers to summon him.

95.   The *muruva*'s wife, a good woman
      Related her dream again
      "It's bound to be true now"
      She murmured in his ear.

96.   He put aside the clothes he wore
      He'd dressed like a demon from hell
      Ash on his body, and a large beard
      And red hibiscus crowning his head.[1]

97.   Dressed in a showy turban
      The curls from his wig falling o'er
      With his hell rod in his hand
      He was dressed like a creature from hell.

98.   In this guise went Maruva
      To see the Pandi king
      He fell prostrate on the floor
      Went backward, then faced him

---

1.   The Maruva's demonic disguise is his way of distancing
     himself from the ill omened task he knows he will be
     asked to perform.

99. "Good man I'll give you gifts and position
     Do as I tell you
     If you kill this hard thief
     Maruva, I'll give you gifts and pay."

100 Then the unjust king
     Told Maruva who worshipped him
     "Take away this thief today
     Torture him, cut him up, kill him."

At this point the song style changes and become a rapid invocation to summon demons in exorcism rites, as the temp of the drum beat illustrates:

Den den dena dena
    den denna denan denadena

At the back of the stage right is a Kohombra tree from which hangs the body of Palanga, now "dead" . The maruva is dressed as a Bear, which in many classical cultures is an avatar of the constellation *Ursa Major*. In Egypt *Ursa Major* is the constellation of the god Seth who performs a similar role to that of the maruva. The executioner enters front stage right, Pattini, together with Kali, are front stage left. The tableau is complete with a rest-house situated at the back of the stage left.

Reprise of story, chanted over the drum beat

101. He takes the jeweled, tinkling anklet

   Of the glorious Pattini

   He quickly goes to the city

   Of the noble Pandi king.

102. He goes into the city

   And meets the goldsmith

   Who take the anklet

   And gives it to the queen.

103. The great king listens

   The beastly smith talks

   O the chief queen said

   "Tell me the worth of my anklet."

104. "The anklet which was lost

   For a very long time

   See it with your own eyes"

   Said the envious goldsmith.

105. To devise a frame-up

   And to destroy a thief in Pandi

   To get money for the anklet

   He went to *maruva* to give him a life.

106. Decked in death's guise
      The hell rod in his right hand
      "I'll take away Palanga
      Kill him and drink his blood, " he thinks.

      Den den dena dena
      den denna denan denadena
      Maruva here you come
      Uttering demon cries
      The world stands aghast
      A demon now comes to do his dance.

Den den dena dena
den denna denan denadena

The death of Palanga is a long drawn out affair and, like Osiris he is eventually killed and dismembered into fourteen pieces. Although, unlike the Egyptian version where details of the killing were deeply taboo, in India these are dramatized. In the late classical astronomical tradition, which was common to Asia and the Near East, the lunar month was divided into two halves of 14 days each. Another schema used by Egyptians divided the lunar month into 30 days. At the beginning of the common era when the myth of Isis travelled internationally, both system were used in Egypt.

In the story, Pattini begins her search for her missing husband, accompanied by her servant, the goddess Kali. This may seem rather surprising, the great goddess Kali reduced to second place next to Pattini. However, within the Buddhist and Jaina world such assimilation and taming of the goddesses of Hinduism was normal.

107. "I've been separated from my husband
       Yet my love for him is still here."
       Crushed by the grief that o'ercame her
       Pattini laments in this manner.

108. "My husband went to trade
       To the city of Madurai
       How far is it to get there
       Tell me Kali-Kodi?"

109. "Then replied Kali-Kodi
       Listen graciously Pattini, O goddess
       You want the distance to the Pandi city
       It is fifty gavu[1] from here."

---

1. A unit of distance. In the story they walk 25 gavu in one day. There are four gavu in a yojana which is 4.5miles. So a gavu is about a mile. In the ancient world a day's march was approximately 25 miles. Obeyesekere comments on how this distance is far enough away to defer the action till the next day.

110. "Like the moon and the hare in its center
     In harmony we lived together
     O my lord exalted
     Why haven't you returned yet?"

111. "Hasn't he yet sold the anklet?
     He's been enticed by another?
     Or has he met with disaster?
     Why has my lord delayed?"

112. Crows sit on the pillars
     Then circle around the house
     Presenting a deadly omen
     They caw flock upon flock.

113. Cows refuse to give milk
     They break loose and scamper
     They shiver when tethered
     And the young calves moan.

114. The sorrows yet to come
     Appeared in deadly signs
     Distraught by fear and doubt
     Pattini suffers in her grief.

115. Gracious Pattini's great love
     Would't leave her breast

Darkness spread over the world
As did her grief.

116. "Unceasingly love shoots his arrows
The gentle wind feels like fire
The cuckoo's tones sound like a demon's
How can I sleep in a lone bed?"

117. "You've left me here one night
Yet it seems like a thousand years
That's how I feel his absence
I can't bear it any longer."

118. Renowned Pattini now sleeps
And in her sleep she dreams
of Palanga, a sword[1] in his hand
It's no sword but his absence.

119. "She prays to the Tender Queens[2]
Permit me to leave today."

---

1. Another bad omen to follow the long list already noted. Indian dream interpretation uses principles very similar to those used in the Egyptian tradition. The sword indicates Palanga has need of one.

2. These are a group of goddesses which seem to be connected with omens and fate?

"I needn't give you permission
Do as your heart tells you."

120. "Oh Sun God shining over the earth
Give me leave to go to Pandi city."
She gets his warrant and approval
She worships all gods and gets their warrant.

121. "To search for my blameless lord
I'll use my full power
How can I be blamed
Let us go now to Pandi city."

122. Sesame cakes and *mun* cakes
Round halvah and milk balls
These she puts in a box
Then she summons Kali.

123. She gives the box to Kali
They travel thirty *gavu*
"Lady, my feet hurt badly"
"If thou canst not, I'll take the box."

124. "What folly is this, woman?
We can't leave this box behind."
"Lady I'll die of weariness
Let's stop under some shade."

Pattini, otherwise stationary,
now moves about the stage.

125. They reach the Velli rest house

A demoness lives there

From the fields below she comes, mouth open

"Today I'll have my prey", she thought.

Enter an actor in demoness costume,
and shrieks of "I'll eat you etc".

126. She comes, mouth open wide

like the plains of the sky

Teeth bared like the bodies of cobras

"How Kali shall we escape today?"

"Lady there's nothing I can say."

127. "Except tie me up as a sacrifice

And I'll expiate my sins."

"Shame Kali, say not so,

I'll display the power of *tejas*."

128. She now raises her little finger[1]

Fire bursts from the four directions

---

1. The little finger is the resting place of elemental fire, from this diminutive location it can grow to become overwhelming. Like Isis, Pattini manifests magical power and sovereignty over serpents.

Then Pattini comes forth
And again raises her little finger.

129. "I'll strike you with plague from head to foot,
Why stand you there? Come into the rest house."
"Lady I cannot raise my feet."
"I order you to come forth here."

130. She [Pattini] loosens her dress and steps back
And "locks" the demoness' mouth and hands
"What ignorant things you do!
What sins you commit by this vagrant life."

131. "Lady how else can I survive?"
[Pattini] "Listen to my angry words,
Take charge of this human world of mine,
Accept processions in Asala (July)."

132. "Accept pujas of horn pulling,
And take my shawl
Yes, you may take my shawl
I'll now name you Madura Mala."

133. "Take charge of my human world,
I go to the land my husband went,
I may never make the return journey,
I will now leave this place."

134. Gracious Pattini now departs
     She reaches the cowherd's street
     "What city is this?" she asks
     From a milkmaid that accosts her.

135. She leaves the street and moves forward
     Cowherders now accost her,
     "Where are you going alone dear girl?"
     "I go in search of my husband."

Pattini's Journey (omitted in some performances)

136. "We shall give you an earring for your ear,
     A precious necklace for your shoulders,
     We shall drape your body in a golden dress
     Tinkling bangles to wear on your arms."

137. "Medallions and toe rings for your feet,
     Silk and gossamer shawls for your waist
     We shall hang curtains and canopies about your bed,
     We shall find a place for you to sleep in this city."

138. "Whatever you say I cannot delay,
     When I meet my husband, I'll rest in bed,
     I follow the path my husband took,
     Though cowherds ask me, I cannot stay."

139. She passed their street and goes afar
    "See how the cowherders abused me
    It's you, lord, who causes all this
    But for this you mustn't get bad karma."

140. She comes to the river Kaveri,
    Its waters - not produced by rain - rushed forth,
    "Why ferryman won't you [thou] ply your trade
    When a woman like me is waiting."

141. "To whom do you jabber thus, wench,
    We don't have women like you in this city,
    We don't ply our boat with the likes of you,
    Women like you don't ride in our boat."[1]

142. "Brother do not abuse me,
    If you want a lass go find one,
    I'll give you money the weight of a lad
    Take it, but row me across."

---

1. A ferryman also plays an obstructive role in an ancient
   Egyptian version of this story, *Contending of Horus & Seth*.
   Tasked by Seth to prevent the goddess Isis crossing over
   to the 'Island in the middle', where a tribunal of the gods
   is deciding on the fate of Horus, the posthumous son of
   Osiris. The ferryman is actually Seth in disguise and thus
   also the brother of Isis and Osiris. The goddess must
   again use magic to get around this obstacle.

143. "What kind of babble is this, wench
      This river is under royal interdict!"
      "Why is it interdict, brother?"
      "I don't know why, nor do I care."

144. She rails at the earth and the sky
      She takes the royal ring in her right hand
      "Which god has caused me this pain?"
      With both hands she throws the gold ring in the river.

145. The waters parted in two above
      The waters parted in two below
      White sands blossomed in between
      And the noble Pattini walks over these.

146. "May pestilence strike the ferryman's kind!"
      The ferryman falls prostrate at her feet
      "Did you not see my might?"
      She calmed his pain and went forth.

147. The parted waters met again,[1]
      With a gunshot sound.

---

1.   The parting of the waters is a feat repeated in many
      Egyptian tales of magic and even makes it into the
      Biblical narrative as the parting of the Red Sea. The
      sudden manifestation of Pattini's wealth and power may

[Asks Kali] "How lady shall we find the ring?"
The ring now fell at her feet.

148. The exalted Pattini goes forth from there,
      She asks people for news of her husband,
      Swiftly sixty gavu pass by,
      That's how she showed her glory.

The drum rhythm changes. This following section is very like a section in the Ramesseum dramatic papyri which describes a similar scene of Isis searching for the corpse of Osiris, calling upon various animals to assist her in the task: "Fish of the deep, fowl of the skies, go seek Osiris where he lies."

149. "O lady bird pecking mango and rose apple and holding them in your beak,
      Kissing your breasts and combing your feathers
      O Cuckoos making sweet melodious sounds
      Quickly say - have you seen my noble lord?"

---

leave the reader pondering on why she had need of human assistance in the first place. An important aspect of ancient story is that the protagonists must be given the chance to do the right thing, if only to reveal their wick-

150. "Nibbling the mango with your sharp parrot teeth
Sucking its juice and enjoying its taste
O flock of parrots hopping from branch to branch
If you've seen my noble lord I'll give you merit."

151. "Stepping out of the woods with your tender babes,
Coyly nudging, eating sweet fruits,
Frolicking in the meadow to please our minds,
O herd of deer, say, if you've seen my noble lord."

152. They've recited their lessons and worshipped
their teacher,
With books in hand in the middle of the street,
"Good children you'll get great merit,
If you show me where his corpse lies."

153. "A handsome noble merchant came to the city,
With an anklet. Do you know if he's been killed?"
she asked.
"Good children you'll get great merit,
If you show me where his corpse lies."

154. "We eagerly went to school in the morning,
We studied the letters and read our books,
Now we are tired and hungry,
Yet we'll show you where he was killed."

155. She gave them sweets and balls of puffed rice,
      Fed them lovingly, gave them water,
      and pleased them,
      She held them close, brushed their hair with her hand,
      And said "Come show me where his body lies."

156. They led her past the city streets,
      And pointed a right hand for Pattini to see,
      Like a cloud seen from beneath a branch,
      They asked her to look under the Margosa's shade.[1]

157. Her dark hair falls over her anguished face,
      Tears stain her breasts,
      She goes up to see her husband's corpse,
      And Pattini weeps in her terrible grief.

158. Pattini the Saint (Muni) arrived there,
      alone in her grief,
      She sees the graceful 'lake body'[2] lying on the ground,

---

1. The Margosa or Neem yields a yellow oil, with disagreeable smell and unpleasant taste. Despite this it has important medicinal properties. The wood contains a high percentage of tannin, and when made into boxes helps preserve the contents from insect attack. In some ways this is the Indian equivalent of Acacia tree that plays a significant role in the mythology of Isis and Osiris.

2. The Neem and now reference to the 'lake body' all reiterate the very Egyptian theme of putrefaction.

Like lightning flashing its colors over
an evening cloud,
Alone in her suffering she embraced her lord's body.

159. The maiden Pattini compassionate, wears a tilaka on
her forehead like a flower,
She places her head against her lord's red lotus feet,
She raises her hands and worships him
again and again,
She cries and cries in her pain of mind and grief.

Then the curse of Pattini on the city of Madurai. In what
follows Pattini sublimates her raw, sexual feelings, long
dammed up and releases this as fiery magical energy, that
she accumulated and releases to burn the city to the ground.

Lamentations of Pattini (and Kali)

160. "Where is that youthful body I created,
O sounder of cuckoo notes,
O warrior mine whom I fed with milk
like the ocean,
O my lotus feet, overflowing with love,
whom I worship,
My own dear lord why has this great pain visited
me?"

161. "Did you rub sandal and rose water on your body
     only to forsake me,
     Did you shed all those tears
     only to go meet Death himself,
     Lord, did you bring the anklet
     only to give it to the Pandi King?
     And did you marry me, lord,
     only to cause me the heat of grief?"

162. "I know why I came here,
     as clearly as I see my face in a mirror,
     Where is my pride if I don't bring you back to life,[1]
     the women of Kaveri will shame me surely,
     By the power of my courage put on your robe lord
     and awake."

163. "The good queen of Pandi had a hand bracelet,
     But the goldsmith lied and falsely killed Palanga,
     My innocent lord, your vital centres destroyed,
     I'll avenge his death, O how can I be consoled?"

---

1. Here one of several references to her resurrecting her
    husband, an unusual theme in Hindu mythology but very
    central to Egyptian religion.

164. "My exalted lord came here,

     But now he's scattered,

     His life extinguished,

     This sin must bear fruit."

165. By the arrow of Benare's king,

     A *kindura*[1] was struck dead,

     This *kindura's* women,

     Had power to bring him back.

166. The god Sakra (Indra) came there,

     "Please protect my husband" she said,

     "May not I have that power,

     I'll show how my power will bear fruit."

167. "Like mercury and gold[2] our minds were bound

     O noble lord, brimming with love,

     How is it that you've left me now,

     By this death you've met?"

---

1. A *kindura* is half human/half peacock. Pattini is evoking ancient precedent, what in classical magic is called a histeriola, a story that somehow enables the subsequent ritual action.

2. Again the idiom is Egyptian, when someone dies that go to meet their Ka. This verse also contains a reference to the mercury and gold of alchemy.

168. "Pale body observe me weep,
     Wake up and open your eyes,
     Wake, wake up now my lord,
     And bring me joy."

169. "At one time in a gay city,
     We enjoyed prosperity together,
     Now there is no turning back,
     Alone without sun and bitter wind."

170. "O my beautiful lord,
     Woe is me my husband dear,
     How like you this 'happiness' now,
     My husband lord of love."

171. "Dazed with love and passion,
     Suffering, I came to this city,
     You lie on this stretch of sand,
     Handsome, my lord awake!"

172. "O downy golden body,
     In the bloom of the Margosa shade,
     No more shawls to lie on,
     Blissfully asleep on those cruel sands."

173. "Tear overbrim, fall over,
     The body burns unceasing,

How could I bear it any longer,
Renowned my lord, awake!"

174. "Can't you hear your girl cry,
Today O lovely one,
Your beauty drawn with brush erased,
Asleep, sprawled in these sands."

175. "I came here in great wrath,
I say these words to you,
'Look!' the power I possess,
My dear husband awake."

176. "Your golden body pales,
By my affection waxes,
My heart throbs painfully,
Lord, I will be revenged."

177. "Husband, sweet of speech,
I took the road you walked,
Why am I thus meek?
Could I bring you back to life?"

Song of Red Rice

178. "In the blazing sun,

     Without a shade,

     O Lord you're in the sun,

     Your corpse is also here."

179. "Have you sown *red rice* (*rattana*)

     To give to flies and worms?

     Why live in a watch hut,

     If one remains silent?"

180. "One lights a fire,

     Two raise the flames,

     To quell this fire,

     Two others pour water."

181. "When there's a slashed swidden[1] (*Chena*),

     An unslashed swidden catches fire,

     It is another swidden,

     If you know, lord tell me?"

182. "The rising floodwater,

     Spreads like an echo,

     Is there any solace,

     For my great pain?"

---

1.   Slash & burn field management.

183. "Why should you like lime,
     If you have an orange?
     Shouldn't you use unripe lime,
     If it's needed for a *nasna* ?"[1]

184. "It's I who asked you,
     To go a-trading,
     I ask you again,
     Do come back and trade."

Palanga is revived

185. Thus she related the virtues,
     Of her beloved husband,
     Crying and sobbing and sobbing,
     'Twas to Pattini's glory.

186. Her virtue spread o'er the world
     Her power germinated
     Mount Meru became warm
     And warm Sakra's (Indra's) jewel throne.

187. Indra was living there,
     in full happiness,

---

1. A medical analogy, a *nasma* is a nasal infusion. These are all related to her attempts to revive Palanga.

When his seat grew warm,
He wanted to know why.

188. He (or she) created an ambrosia pond,
Wetted the shawl with its water,
Placed a hand on Palanga's head,
And told him to get up.

189. As if lying in a bed,
Deep in cool sleep,
By the influence of Pattini,
The Prince rose joyous.

190. God Indra (Sakra) then,
Pleasantly said
"To please Pattini
Palanga now rise."

191. O the great fatigue she suffered!
The power of her *tejas!*
Bring a singing priest,
Utter the "resurrection" and calm the fire.

192. "I shall now show the might of my *tejas,*
On my good husband's behalf,

I shall display my full power,

As I am a Pattini[1] for this world."

Final Valedictory Song

193. How Pattini showed her might,

    In this manner, to the world,

    Its golden sound spread confusion,

    As she threw the anklet on this slab of earth.

194. The sound of the spreading anklet,

    Shook the blood of those near and far,[2]

    The king hid in fear,

    His blood shook from the mouth below.

195. Grabbing the gold from the people,

    And leading a deceitful life,

    O cunning goldsmiths,

    Why do you kill the innocent?

---

1. Again Pattini is referred to in the generic sense as one of a
    class of supernatural beings.

2. Again, like Isis, Pattini has a fearsome aspect. In the
    Egyptian myth Isis several times kills humans around her
    who happen to have gotten on the wrong side of her or
    simply because they are in the vicinity when she releases
    her destructive side.

196. Ignorant of royal dhamma,[1]

     lacking in foresight,

     Committing iniquity, not rightness,

     King what canst thou do now?

197. "What do you want O wife of the anklet thief?

     I'll tear off your breast and make you eat it."

     "Why do I need my tainted breast any longer?"

     She broke it and threw its golden plate.

198. As it struck, the city burst into flame,

     If you say 'tis false your mouth will smart,

     Such is the strength of the goddess Pattini,

     The palace became a mound of ashes.

Pattini tears off her breast, rather a brutal offering, a remembrance of Palanga's tender squeeze of her breasts before he set out on his ill fated quest. Otherwise the significance is obscure, perhaps as a reverse fertility symbol. Some see a parallel in the ancient Egyptian posture of mourning in which female relatives hold their breasts. This association is extremely old and is evident in pre-dynastic anthropoid pots found in ancient Coptos. Their hands cup their breasts (see picture). One of the emblems of Isis is the breast shaped pot known as a situla, which she uses to pour libations.

---

1. Sanskrit: Dharma, "Duty".

The city is burned, only the good queen, the people, Buddhist temples, monks and relics are spared.

199.   Divine Sata, who saw this event, said thus:

"Pattini cause no more suffering."

He implored Pattini with his hands on his forehead,

"Cause no more pain and human deaths."

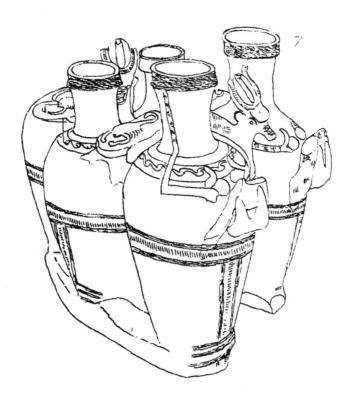

Source: W. M. Flinders, Hogarth, David George (1896) Koptos.

200.　Thus King Sata bowed before her
　　　And asked her to stop the fire soon
　　　"I destroyed the Pandi king and evil people only
　　　Did you not see, sire this yourself?"

201.　She spoke thus to King Sata.
　　　She said she'd stop the fire.
　　　"If you give me tribute of drums,
　　　Then I'll end this conflagration."

A Cow is sacrificed to make a drum, then is resurrected

202.　So the cow got up at once again,
　　　The calf [who suffered from its mother's death],
　　　Could now pull at the udder,
　　　With the calf near her, the cow could now give milk.

203.　Following the instructions of old teachers,
　　　They milked the cow and poured the milk in a pot,
　　　They built a fire-pit (*torana*) in the right manner,
　　　And boiled milk outside for the Sun God.

204.　Thus they performed it as she'd wished
　　　Sweet-smelling flowers were offered all day,
　　　Beautiful leaves of Betel were also offered,
　　　And milk boiled in front of each household.

205. And so she brought happiness to the world,
   She created a pond of ambrosia that day,
   She wetted the end of her shawl with it,
   brought blessings on all by fanning.[1]

Spell for cooling of heat or of fire

206. Then the gods assembled in their glory
   They showered glorious "rain flowers" from the sky
   As if a roaring river was falling
   That's how the Madura fire was quenched.

207. Having quenched the fire, she stayed
   for a while there,
   That a second calamity might not befall the city,
   She quenched the flames with compassion,
   And departed then for the Veli rest house.

---

1. This kind of sacrifice is very archaic. The sacrifice and resurrection of a cow and the mention of the calf brings to mind similar rites in Egypt where cattle sacrifice was common. Seth, the murderer of Osiris is made to carry the corpse on his back, and in some accounts is then sacrificed. Earlier we described similar offerings of rice pudding (pongala) made every year in honour of the goddess.

Pattini's apotheosis

208. She saw the chariot that was sent and was pleased,
    She prayed for a Buddhahood to come soon,
    With thoughts of compassion
    and the observance of precepts,
    She went away in the chariot that was sent.

The other gods have intervened and successfully appeal to her to stop the destruction. In return Pattini is promised that after fourteen days she will again see Palanga, resurrected in astral form.

Afterwards she enters a monastery, meditates and reaches nirvana. Unlike Isis, she has no offspring. However her "sister" Madhavi gives birth to a *surrogate* daughter called Manimekalai, who is the subject of another classic of Tamil literature. Madhavi was the beautiful courtesan whose relationship with Pattini's husband Palanga precipitated the financial crisis that set the story in motion.

This story of Manimekalai, full of magic, concludes with her conversion to Buddhism. Essentially it chronicles the emergence of a new kind of religious identity for women, one that lies somewhere between traditional roles of whore or mother. This third way, is of female religious practitioner, what we might called a nun. So not quite the same as Horus who represents in ancient Egypt the new form of kingship. Even so it is some new synthesis that arises in this narrative.

Conclusion

The late classical cult of Isis famously spread to the far corners of the globe. I hope I have drawn you into an interesting and largely unknown tale of how the cult arrived in India. Its introduction in the early centuries of the common era also corresponds with many new innovations in Hinduism. One that I find particularly interesting is the rise of what we in the West call *Tantra*. I would argue that Tantra is a magical religion. Magic was also the religion of ancient Egypt. It is my contention through this and other research, that there is much common ground between both traditions. Isis was of course celebrated as a goddess "great of magick", so the connection between both realms may be quite deep.

Pattini, as we learn through the myth cycle is no ordinary mortal. She has knowledge of magic which she uses in her quest. She is also said to be from a special order of supernatural beings - literally she is a Pattini. A Pattini is perhaps comparable to a class of supernaturals known in Sanskrit as Yoginis. Even the existence of these beings was a great secret until revealed by the work of some intrepid researcher. Their shrines are different to those of classical Hinduism, definitely off the map and off the grid. Special spaces whose openness to the sky facilitates their descent into the temple.

The goddess Isis is especially loved by women who find spiritual and worldly liberation in her cult. In Kerala, the region of India into which her cult was transmitted, the status of women is higher than elsewhere in India. Dianne Jenett (1998) whose work we have referenced several times writes:

"... In 1987, I observed the relative equality and free agency of women as contrasted with my impressions of women in other parts of India. Kerala has strong and living traditions of matrilineality, serpent groves, and the goddess Bhadrakala. Those traditions, combined with Malayati (nomenclature for people from Kerala, from the language, Malayalam) tolerance for religious and social diversity, prompted me to speculate on what cultural beliefs unique to Kerala may have contributed to the differences. Kerala, the source of spices for thousands of years, has been washed by wave after wave of religious and social ideas carried by traders but has never been invaded or occupied, so new ideas and religions were incorporated, layer after layer, into the existing culture."[1]

I'd also add that the status of women was higher in Egypt than in any other part of the ancient world. It was in a sense

---

1. Dianne Jenett "Red Rice for Bhagavati" *ReVision*, Winter 1998 v20 : 7

the last bastion of feminine power that in remote antiquity, had doubtless been even higher.

Enough clues exist to re-enact this ritual in your own temple. There is an elaborate story to retell, a drum rhythm to accompany the singing of the mantras and a simple ritual food offering to make and share.

Den den dena dena
    den denna denan denadena

Index